Listening for the Holy Good

Listening for the Holy Good

Readings for Personal Retreat and Meditation

MARIE E. GIBSON

RESOURCE *Publications* • Eugene, Oregon

LISTENING FOR THE HOLY GOOD
Readings for Personal Retreat and Meditation

Resource Publications
An Imprint of Wipf and Stock Publishers
199 W. 8th Ave., Suite 3
Eugene, OR 97401

www.wipfandstock.com

PAPERBACK ISBN: 979-8-3852-6923-5
HARDCOVER ISBN: 979-8-3852-6924-2
EBOOK ISBN: 979-8-3852-6925-9

VERSION NUMBER 01/21/26

All poetry was written by Marie E. Gibson. The *Strawberry Island Poems* are from two chapbook collections of poetry written during a retreat on Strawberry Island within Lake Simcoe in Ontario, Canada. The island retreat center was then owned by the Basilian Fathers. “If Jesus Wrote Poems” is part of a Lenten meditation chapbook, *Jesus as Poet: From Life to Passion*.

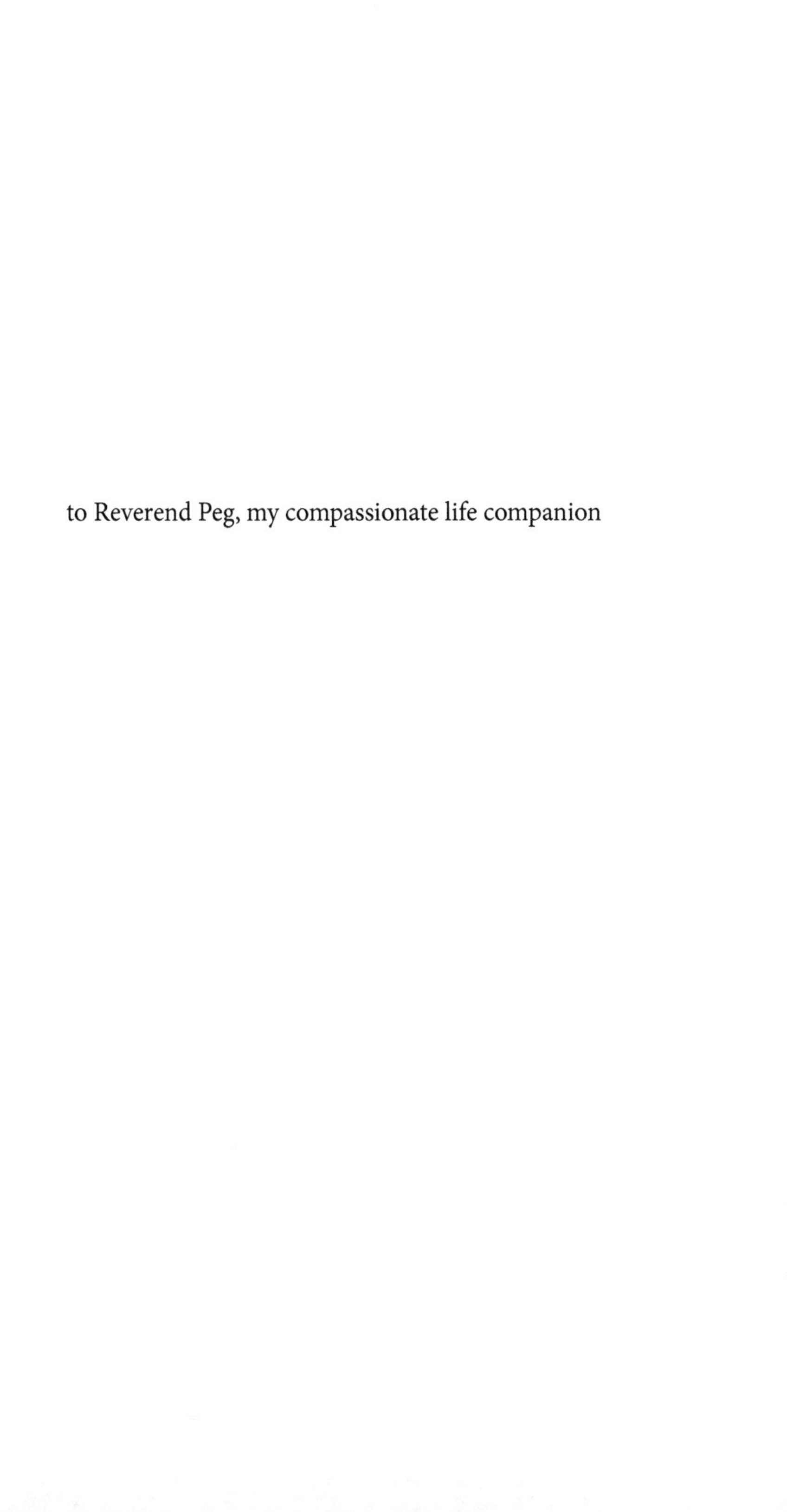

to Reverend Peg, my compassionate life companion

Contents

List of Poems

Introduction

As I finished a two-year program of spiritual direction with the Episcopal Diocese of Rochester and Morningstar Ministries, I found myself increasingly using metaphor to explain my inner presence of God. Being the only liberal Presbyterian in the class of Episcopalians, Roman Catholics, and one conservative Methodist, I constantly battled against the conception of God as "He" and defended my understanding of the Holy Spirit as "She," whom I had also come to know as "Sophia," the Greek understanding of holy wisdom. Each of our experiences of God differed, not entirely due to our denominational traditions, but rather to our personal experiences of the Holy. Together we studied the academics of spirituality; however, I recognized the spirit of God in elements of life that were more diverse than the written word. Might my unique way of seeing God in the world be helpful to others?

There is no one word that is complete enough to express God—the Holy Good. Neither popes, nor saints, nor any other holy leaders can define fully your personal and creative expression of God.

Pondering these thoughts, I was reminded of the book *Seven Years in Tibet* by Heinrich Harrer. He is asked by the 14th Dalai Lama to build a small movie theatre, and he is told to wait several days before beginning work so the monks can find all the worms in the plot of earth and move them to a safer place. It is an act of compassion, and it becomes Harrer's holy time of waiting. As peculiar as some experiences may seem, our sacred moments often come at times when we are called to stop what we are doing and wait. We take these moments, wait and observe, then recognize the holiness in them. This waiting and observing must be intentional on our part.

My hope is that *Listening for the Holy Good* will offer you opportunity for waiting and observing, giving insight into ordinary moments, and giving you a time of stillness and peace in the middle of the day as you set aside anxiety or frustration or perhaps even boredom. This might be a book to reach for at the end of the day to forget or to unwind before drifting into sleep. The poems are offered to help in your spiritual centering and meditation. Observe how the words settle in your mind. If a thought or image comes to you, sit quietly and let your heart rest in it. You might want to do a "lectio divina" (divine reading) to see if it helps you listen, sense, or feel "the Holy Good," or take some time to journal your thoughts and experience.

I believe the Holy Good will emerge in all its profound mystery in more unlikely places and unique ways when you stop, listen, and observe where you are at any given time or place. Expand your conception of the Holy, and find God everywhere, in every moment.

MEG

Just under the surface I shall be, all together at first, then separate and drift, through all the earth and perhaps in the end through a cliff into the sea, something of me. A ton of worms in an acre, that is a wonderful thought, a ton of worms, I believe it.

—Samuel Becket, *From an Abandoned Work*

On Being All One

It was seven in the evening on June 16th when I finished mowing the lawn. The air was cool and felt soothing on my warm, moist skin. The earlier part of the day was filled with studies on St. Benedict, St. Augustine, John Cassian, Teresa of Avila, John of the Cross, and many profundities of the ancient mystics. I had applied to take an educational leave from my position as executive director of the Greater Rochester Community of Churches to follow my call to spiritual direction. The course was given by Morningstar Ministries under the oversight of the Episcopal Diocese of Rochester. It was a two-year program with two sets of intensive nine-day studies including a long weekend silent retreat after each session. I was on the eighth day of my second year of intensive study and my mind and body were overflowing—like a bucket with holes in it and water streaming out everywhere. As the water flows out, the bucket gets lighter, gratefully for the one who is carrying it. Overflowing endeavors like these lead me to respite work in my yard. There's nothing better than mowing the lawn—uphill—to forget or perhaps to understand the great mystics and their often stress-filled lives.

As I finished my chore and was returning to the back deck, I noticed in my neighbor's yard a robin hopping down a pathway. It hopped a few steps, stopped, cocked its head as though listening, and then pecked at the dirt and grass. It then hopped a few more steps, stopped, cocked its head in the other direction, and pecked again at the dirt and grass. This went on for a minute or so and I was mesmerized with its behavior. It was as though the robin was listening for worms and could tell where they were hiding.

Listening for worms is about as reasonable a thing to do as listening to one hand clapping. In *The Zen Master Hakuin: Selected Writings*[1] it is said when you clap together both hands a sharp sound is heard; when you raise the one hand there is neither sound nor smell. This wisdom is from a Mahayana koan (riddle), and I'm not sure what the lack of sound has to do with the lack of smell, yet it is a greater part of the mystery. Although birds do have olfactory senses, they rarely use them to find food. As for making sounds, I could not find any conclusive information that worms, when in the presence of a robin, would call out in some frightful manner as to attract attention to themselves.

I came to no thorough conclusion about the episode of the robin that seemed to be listening for worms except that the bird did seem satiated when it finally flew away. I, on the other hand, was still exhausted and sat for a while to rest and think about my few moments of entertainment, or perhaps, as it might have been, enlightenment.

The studies of the day were of the Christian mystics. A particular favorite of mine is Meister Eckhart, born around 1260 in eastern Germany, around the lifetime of Thomas Aquinas. Eckhart joined the Dominican Order of Preachers and emulated the life of an Apostle of Jesus. He eventually served as professor, preacher, and spiritual leader in the Rhineland. It was a place and time of visions and mystical experiences. It seemed to me that Eckhart had taken the mystery of God and peeled it like an onion, until when he reached the center, he found himself and what he called the "Godhead" to be one. He uses the phrase "the spark of the soul" to describe that very mystical closeness.[2] He says, "If we could only

1. Ekaku, "Yabukoji," 164.
2. Eckhart, *Essential Sermons*, 230.

have space to hear, we would be awestruck. Silence allows God to awaken our consciousness."[3]

If we could only have *space to hear*, perhaps we might be able to listen for worms. Perhaps the most silent of all creatures would be heard shouting for joy, or in the case of this little worm that was being pursued by the robin, shouting for *fear,* but nonetheless being heard. After all, it is often in our moments of fear, rather than joy, that we long to be heard.

Perhaps the lesson of the listening robin, in a mystical way, is just another experience of God showing us that to hear the sound of the worm, we must listen very carefully in the midst of our hopping around. To *listen*, one must be silent. A wise communications professor once said, "Are you listening, or waiting to talk?"

So in the cool of the early evening I sit and listen. I hear a robin perched high on a telephone wire at the edge of my freshly mown lawn. It sings a melodic song of joy, as I do believe that it and the worm are now one.

3. Eckhart, *Essential Sermons*, 205.

THE PROCESS OF SITTING

(A Strawberry Island Poem)

I sit.
I think.
I listen.
I sit.
I listen.
I sit.
What does it take
to get me here
to the point of
just sitting?
Even now a small
bee hums about the
tip of my pen;
A chickadee sings
her cheerful tune in
the majesty of the wind,
who plays the tops of trees
like I play my guitar.
Even now the lake and sky
call to me;
"Come and play!"
No, not now.
For in this moment
I sit;
It is all I am
called to do.

Red sky at night—sailor's delight. Red sky in morning—sailor's warning.

—TRADITIONAL SAYING

Signs

I'M A FIRM BELIEVER in signs. I think we are all challenged by signs every day of our lives, but rarely do we notice them. It's not until something hits us head on that we suddenly recognize a sign.

Some signs are obvious, as in the saying above. A beautiful red sunset usually is followed by a clear night, while a striped pink haze in the morning will usually bring rain. When the wind blows the back of the leaves exposing their silvery sides it often portends a storm. People say the more wooly the caterpillar, the heavier the winter. Watching the geese fly in flight formation to the south in November tells me winter is on its way. Watching the geese fly north in March tells me that Ol' Man Winter will soon take his leave.

I was born into a superstitious home in which signs were a way of life. My grandfather was a Sicilian from a poor agricultural family that worked the farmland of his town. When he came to the United States in the early 1900s, he continued to work farmland for several years in the onion fields of Elba, New York. The earth was in his blood and he seemed to understand the signs of life around him. He could grow things in his backyard that were not meant to thrive in the cold northeast climate. Every fall I would help him put the fig tree to sleep for the winter by bending it down toward the ground and covering it with old wool coats and blankets. In the spring, we would uncover it, stake it, and watch it bloom with beautiful white blossoms that would gift us with the most luscious deep purple figs I ever tasted. My grandfather was a man of few words, and the signs of life seemed reflected in his observant dark eyes.

My grandmother was born to immigrant Italians who lived at the turn of the twentieth century near the border of New York State and Pennsylvania. She knew other signs—religious and mystical signs, like when someone was going to die, or when a baby would be born. Depending on how the mother carried the baby in her womb, she knew if it was a boy or girl. She also believed, as many women do even today, that insufferable indigestion meant the baby would be born with lots of hair. Members of the family would come to my grandmother complaining of headaches. She would perform a ritual. If drops of oil in water held over the person's head gathered in one large clump, the person had received the "evil eye." I'm not sure what ritual was performed to remove the "evil eye," but I know that prayer was involved.

The women in my family would gather around my grandmother's kitchen table, drink coffee, smoke cigarettes, and talk about mysterious experiences. There was the time a relative was dying in an upstairs bedroom and family members had come to pay their last respects. It was summer and windows were open. A bird flew into the kitchen, circled around the ceiling and flew back out. At that moment, it was said, the relative died. My grandmother said the bird was the person's soul taking flight.

It stands to reason that I grew up a highly intuitive person attuned to the evidence of signs in my life. I was nine months pregnant with my firstborn child when I woke early on a Wednesday morning in December and went into the bathroom. Sunlight was streaming through the frosted window and reflected off the mirror bouncing an image of light on the yellow wall. It was in the shape of a cross, and I knew my baby would be born that day. I went into labor and later that evening my daughter was born. The mystery of all the indigestion I had endured during those nine months became evident as I admired the shock of black hair on the top of her tiny head, now combed into a finger curl by the midwife.

Another experience I recall occurred just before I had to leave the house for work one day. For some reason I decided to go out the back door instead of the front. I armed the house, pulled the door open and stopped. There on the deck railing post, proud and still, was a peregrine falcon. It was so close I could see its keen deep brown eyes watching me. It barely turned its head toward me, unconcerned with my presence. I studied it—the soft brown gray of its feathers, the strip of dark over its eye, and how its beak seemed rather small for such a bird of prey. I was mesmerized. I wanted to remember every line, every pattern. We were inches apart, watching one another for a good minute until the house alarm system began to emit a quick series of beeps. The bird lifted up from the wooden post and disappeared into the dull gray morning sky. I stepped out of the doorway in the nick of time, closing the door before the alarm went off.

Such encounters and stories can be sloughed off or we can recognize them as signs and messages within our life. Each of us is called to see signs, listen for signs, and feel signs—the sky, the wind, the plants and birds, the phases of the moon. Even the signs I see in people—their movements, proclivity in speech, the distance in their gaze, their intent on being in the moment or their mind distracted and a million miles away. These signs open the door to their being in this life—in this moment. These signs open the door for us all to see beyond the ordinary.

With signs, life teaches and forewarns us. What is conjured up in our minds when we think of the full moon? Be wakeful, as the poet Rumi says, in "Search the Darkness":

> Be a wakeful candle in a golden dish,
> Don't slip into the dirt like quicksilver.
> The moon appears for night travelers,
> Be watchful when the moon is full.[1]

1. Helminski, *Pocket Rumi Reader*, 42.

SPIDER IN THE CHAPEL

(A Strawberry Island Poem)

White stucco walls
and pine wooden pews;
a clay floor that nestles
with patterned bricks in
a soft gray hue.
Sunlight sifts its way
through the rain-spotted
glass and comes to rest
upon a spun-white thread
of web suspended from
the top of the arched wood
plank ceiling, like a tapestry
of fine craftsmanship.
There in the middle teeters
the small, firm black dot of
its owner, clutched like a
bull's eye to a scalloped face.
The spider guards this chapel's
holy place, dangling over the
plain, bare altar, it does not
falter in its reverence as it
has come to take a turn
at being sacred.

I hear and I forget, I see and I remember,
I do and I understand.

—Chinese Proverb attributed to Confucius

Miracle at 103

The time had come for me to sell my house. This was the home where I had raised my three children. It was a Cape Cod on a double city lot on the north side of the city, one block from the Great Lake of Ontario. Neighbors used to tease one another saying if the taxes got any higher we would annex to Canada.

It was a great place to raise children, especially as a single mother. There were neighbors on all sides that looked after us when we most needed it. There were jars of homemade jelly left on the step, fresh tomatoes, cucumbers, and zucchini during the summer months. The driveway was plowed in the winter when snow was as high as the doorsteps. There was a park and a baseball field, an elementary school, a high school, and several churches of various denominations all within walking distance. And of course, there was the beautiful lake. It was a perfect location to live one's life quietly, safely, and away from what sometimes seemed a threatening world.

But the time had come. The children had grown and left home. It was just me, a big yellow lab named Ollie, and the ornery tabby cat, Sophie. I had been alone for thirteen years and had finally met someone I trusted and loved and with whom I was once again ready to share my life. My new companion helped me tackle the insurmountable task of cleaning out every nook and cranny from basement to dormer, repainting, and preparing the house for new owners. I wasn't asking a great deal of money, and it was a "buyer's market." And now the house wasn't selling. It sat empty for several months.

In my Sicilian Catholic background there are certain rituals that one practices for "favors from the saints." Praying to St. Anthony for lost objects and to St. Jude for the impossible task was not unreasonable. A St. Joseph's Table would be offered with food and sweets and fruits from all the cousins and relatives in thanks for prayers answered to heal a family member. My Aunt Jean said novenas and we all lit candles for all kinds of reasons. So what do you do if you want to sell a house? You call upon St. Joseph.

The ritual consists of taking a statue of St. Joseph and burying it in the front lawn of the property you want to sell. Somewhere in my memory was the idea that burying the statue upside down would "seal the deal." The only statue of St Joseph I had belonged to my grandmother, and it was a very special keepsake. I didn't want to bury that in the dirt. Since I worked in the faith community and had access to a great many nuns and sisters, I went to our local convent to buy a small plastic statue of St. Joseph.

To my dismay, there were no little plastic St. Joseph statues to be found. There were so many houses for sale that summer I was sure all the St. Josephs were already buried. I wondered if people who do excavation and construction work ever unearth these little statues and what they do with them. It might be profitable for someone to start a "used statue" business. At any rate, I was out of luck and would just have to continue to be patient and wait.

Each day I waited for a sign from God. Each day I waited for a phone call from the realtor. And each day I waited for news that someone had a little plastic St. Joseph to offer as sacrifice to my petition. Fortunately, I worked in a church and my office was just a few steps from the sanctuary. One day, in a moment of great impatience and with great determination, I left my desk and made my way to the altar where a stone statue of Jesus stood, his arms outstretched as he had been for many years, looking down upon petitioners, maybe some just like me. I looked up and said, "Jesus! I am so tired of waiting for my house to be sold and I can't find a statue of St. Joseph to bury in the front yard. Since St. Joseph must be preoccupied with all the other people who have buried his likeness in their yards, could you please help me sell my house?"

With a big sigh, I turned my back on the stone Jesus and looked out over the sanctuary, thinking of the many people who sit in these pews with far more serious prayers and who wait patiently, or maybe impatiently, for Holy attention. I made my way back to my office and sat down feeling discouraged. This house had been my home and sanctuary for so long. Was there not someone in the city that needed this home to offer comfort and safety to their family as it had mine?

About an hour later the phone rang.

It was my realtor. She had a buyer for the house. It was a single mother who had a child recovering from cancer and she wanted a little house like mine to raise and care for him through his treatments. She would pay me exactly my asking price. We made a date to sign papers. I hung up the phone and tears welled in my eyes.

In his book *The Mountain of Silence: A Search for Orthodox Spirituality,* Kyriacos C. Markides talks about his experience with his friend and spiritual guide, Father Maximos, from Mount Athos Monastery in Cyprus. In a community where miracles were everyday occurrences, Father Maximos would say, "Remember, whatever good or bad things happen to us, they have only one single purpose, to awaken us to the reality of God and help us on the path toward union with Him."[1] "Further more," he said, ". . . take heart that nothing happens in the world outside of God's providential will, though it must forever remain a mystery to human reason."[2]

It was a mystery of human reason for me that the house at 103 sold to a young woman who, much like myself, longed for the respite of a place to call home during a time of transition in her family's life. Here she would raise her son surrounded by the possibility of many other little miracles that, as I had come to know, make life a little like heaven on earth.

1. Markides, *Mountain of Silence*, 77.
2. Markides, *Mountain of Silence*, 52.

DOUBT

In the darkness, last night
before I fell to sleep
I felt the heart of Christ
beat deep inside my chest.
Could this be where the
Soul was laid to rest?
I whisper,
"Do not let my mind
forget you."
A slit of light moves
slowly across the ceiling
and an echo of words
replies,
"You cannot keep
Yourself from me; I am
Who you will always be."

We've flown free from their fangs,
free of their traps, free as a bird.
Their grip is broken;
we're free as a bird in flight.

—Ps 124:7 (MSG)

Birds of a Feather

It's October and the trees in the city are turning yellow and red. Some of the Sycamore leaves have dried early from the lack of rain and they scurry in the wind through the street making rattle-like sounds. It's still amazingly warm for autumn in New York. And thank goodness, for I have noticed in the backyard, among the many plain brown birds (known in some birding communities as PBBs), a bright yellow and green parakeet.

When I first encountered this rare beauty in the open expanse of the outdoors, I noticed the PBBs would shun it. They darted at this stranger and pecked it away from the feeder. But after a few days of being together in their feathered community, they seemed more welcoming to the interloper. I called the "pretty bird" Sam.

Sam would sit quietly in the background of the overgrown mock orange tree, which gave him a safe haven from the startling threats of larger birds and curious neighborhood cats. When the PBBs had their fill of seed, Sam would fly over and eat. A few brave little finches would stay the course and join in the meal.

Sam loomed large over most of the other birds, even though they seemed more aggressive and mean-spirited. He waddled his way into their lives and day by day managed to get his way at the feeder and in the lineup on the telephone wire.

At first I worried about Sam. He was in the wild, so to speak; much wilder than his cage in the home of some worried owner who now wondered where their bird had flown. I thought about where he slept at night. On a tree limb? In a rain spout? In the gnarl of a tree?

One day, in a fit of needing to rescue the parakeet, I went to the pet store and bought a small inexpensive bird cage, foolishly thinking the bird would see it and seek shelter. Why ever would Sam choose metal bars and a tiny swing over blazing colorful trees and long sturdy branches? Yet still, I brought the cage home and set it up on the back deck.

Each morning and late afternoon I would see the PBBs enhanced by the bright yellow glow of Sam's wings. One morning he even hung upside down off the telephone wire and watched his comrades enjoy their breakfast. "He's a clown," I mused. Sam dropped from his circus act and joined the others birds for a well-earned meal. I heard the rustle of little feathers from the audience of onlookers. Sam seemed to project that loveable amusing character—the backyard show-off.

The yellow parakeet was relishing a new way of life, but it was not the way of his ancestors born in the warm comfort of the tropics. I began to worry he would not make it through the coming winter months. Maybe he would find a flock of migrating birds and fly south. Maybe he would decide to adjourn to life in the bird cage again. I kept the cage in a safe place on the back deck filled with seed, just in case he made what I considered a wise decision, to flee paradise.

Sam continued to bask in the warm autumn months and remained his yellow perky bird-self. But eventually the biting winds whipped in from Canada and the nights dropped into the teens. Many of the birds in the yard flew south. Sam disappeared.

Some chickadees and house finches continued to sit on the telephone wire and frequent the feeder. The large crows sat at the tops of the pines as they do, so as to announce impending danger. But I never saw Sam again. I thought he might return in the spring, but he did not. Cold and exhaustion could very well have been his demise. He might have dropped unnoticed with the yellow leaves and been covered over by the first snow fall. He is like a golden jewel in my memory now.

Much like in the lives we are all called to live, Sam made choices that for some might have seemed foolish. And yet for others they might have seemed the best choices ever—the only ones possible. The choice to live brightly and boldly and maybe even foolishly among the plainer birds of the world was the best way to utilize the fullness of the time given to Sam. And it was God's sweet gift to me.

DINNER GUEST

(A Strawberry Island Poem)

Lines of two stand at either side
of the serving tables; plates in hand
we examine our sustenance
and eye our desserts.
Clinking dishes, taps of silverware
mingle with low chatter against a
backdrop of humming ceiling fans.
Then, cutting through the monotones
of somewhat insignificant drones
comes a thin, clear sound;
a little chirping, if you will—
from a small, gentle cliff swallow
who has come to sit on the railing
outside the screen door.
She seems to ask nothing of anyone;
no food, no praise.
Sit she does, smooth with azure
head and sparkling eyes, wings still
and at her side, asking nothing more
than for someone to hear her song.

You must not blame me if I do talk to the clouds, . . .

—Henry David Thoreau, *Familiar Letters*

Cloud People

The cloud people are in the sky tonight. You know the ones I mean; white forms that billow over a light gray sky and move across the horizon in a parade of imaginative creatures. Tonight there are two mourning doves sitting side by side and a clown paddling by in a canoe.

The amazing thing about cloud people is that they are as creative as they are bizarre. They are ever changing. If they don't want to be a clown paddling by in a canoe, they turn into a flock of ducks on the ocean or a bear lying on his back with his paws up in the air.

I love the skies in early September. They are exotic and dynamic. It's the time of year when western New York is clothed in changing weather patterns from the Great Lakes and a noticeable chill comes down from Ontario, Canada. There are days of light wispy feather clouds and rippling stratus clouds that resemble the ridges of sand at the beach after the tide recedes. There are great hovering cumulus clouds that move over the cooling earth creating equally as mesmerizing shadows over the hills and meadows, and over the roofs of city homes. There are the deep blue cloudless skies that rise with the morning sun and remain clear until one tiny little soul of a cloud makes its way across the azure backdrop. It's like a refugee seeking a family, journeying ever on until it folds into a night sky, consumed by a blanket of dark blue velvet.

You can see these images in your mind's eye. Clouds are like the Earth's Etch-A-Sketch for people of all ages. If you're bored or lonely, or if you are fearful or angry, clouds are there for you. If you are joyful or in love, clouds will enhance your bliss. Whatever your sense is of the present moment, you can expand it by merely looking up at the sky. Clouds are always there, in all kinds of weather and at all times of the day. Even when people say "there's not a cloud in the sky," somewhere, someplace perhaps out of your view, there is a cloud passing by.

Sometimes at night I will hear the wind tapping on the balcony door. I'll step out into the darkness, and there up above I find thousands of little quips of clouds lit up by an invisible moon. The wind will blow these little puffs along at such a clip, they seem to me like an ancient army of cloud people marching in regalia. I particularly like watching the night sky when I can see billows of white drift by against a washed-out gray backdrop in patchy clusters, moving slowly like a gigantic turtle shell.

I often begin my cloud viewing at dusk, when the edges of the sky are tinted in yellow and rose hues. The day ends like an angel turning the dimmer switch in her living room to the very lowest point, maybe five watts. There! I can see her nestled in her recliner, head back against a cushion, gazing out and maybe looking for the first star of the night. Slowly, the light fades and she disappears and I am standing once again alone with a small pang of desire left inside my soul, wondering when I will once again see the angel.

FLOW

(A Strawberry Island Poem)

The water flows,
between the stems of green
it flows;
past village, cliffs and dodging swallows
it flows;
over rocks and under wooden docks
it flows;
under the lofty wings of the cormorant and loons
it flows;
cutting through the warm morning air
it flows;
The water flows beyond our days and time;
it does not wait but continues cleansing our lives,
yours and mine,
mingling,
tingling,
and even blending us together;
it flows.

You, god . . . who lives next door;
If at times, through the long night, I trouble you with
my urgent knocking—this is why: I hear you breathe
so seldom. I know you're all alone in that room. . . .
I wait listening, always. Just give me a sign!

—Rainer Marie Rilke, *Book of Hours*

Calling On a Saint

It was New Year's Eve. Just after midnight I called my son in New York City to wish him a Happy New Year. I caught him and his companion on the return ferry trip to Staten Island. "So . . . did you have a good evening?" I asked.

"Oh Mom . . . don't ask!" was his woeful reply. He went on to tell me that they were returning from a party in the harbor area. They wanted to catch the ferry home and it was just ready to leave. They found themselves running through the gates and charging up the dock just before the boat left. Catching their breath as they sat down, he reached for his wallet. It was missing. He retraced his steps through the boat and found nothing. "It must have slipped out of my jacket as we were running to catch the ferry," he said.

I felt bad for him and questioned, "Did you have a lot of money in it?"

"No . . . just two twenty-dollar bills. And it's not the money. It's my credit card and my license and my social security card."

I tried to cheer him up. "Well, the best thing that could happen is that someone will find the wallet and bring it back to you."

"No, Mom. The best thing is if it fell into the Hudson River and is never found. I don't want anyone using my I.D."

With that dismal remark I replied, "I'll light my St. Michael candle and ask that your wallet be returned to you and that someone will leave you one of those twenty-dollar bills." He sighed a doubtful chuckle. We exchanged our New Year's wishes and love. I hung up the phone and went to find the St. Michael candle.

I came across these vigil candles in the supermarket aisle with the Hispanic foods. I love the candles. They're colorful and they remind me of my Aunt Jean who was a devout Italian Catholic and prayed novenas to the saints. She was a tiny woman who called me honey and had that popular painting of the blue-eyed Jesus face on the wall with eyes that followed me around the room. So I always had to be good while I was in Aunt Jean's house.

As I lit the candle that night I told St. Michael all about what had happened to my son, knowing, of course, he probably already knew about it. Regardless, it would be a good thing for my son to have a miracle in his life tonight. After all, it was New Year's Eve.

I went to sleep and in the middle of the night the phone rang. I looked up at the illuminated numbers on the clock. Three AM. Someone must have died. "Mom?" I heard my son's voice.

"What's the matter?" I replied, still tucked under my bed covers with the phone to my ear.

"You'll never believe what just happened!" He proceeded to tell me that someone rang his doorbell just a few minutes earlier, and when he opened the door no one was there, but the wallet was on the doorstep. All his papers were still in it. "And guess what, Mom . . . " I couldn't imagine. "There was one twenty-dollar bill in it. Thanks for lighting that candle."

I smiled in the darkness of my room that New Year's Eve and said, "You're welcome, honey. Have a great New Year!" Then I thanked the saint and went back to sleep.

KITE AND MOON

(A Strawberry Island Poem)

She runs, runs, runs and
tosses high the ornamental kite
in this immaculate sky.
And it falls, falls, falls,
trailing way behind
as the kite string twirls and
whirls a cylindrical motion,
making mockery of her devotion;
meditation practice has gone on hold.
Your students stand in awe, we watch
this escapade unfold; lend a hand, no.
Yet giving encouragement and great advice,
to you, who once again tries, tries and tries.
Soon up it rises, higher, higher, higher;
slicing the once rainy-day clouds wide open,
sun barreling down, drying wetness all around,
and there beyond the kite tail that now seems
so far, far, far away, we see the crest of an almost
full moon smiling, beaming down in near
laughter as our joy dances with the high-flying
kite, now launched in its fullness and bloom.

In me there is darkness,
But with you there is light;
I am lonely, but you do not leave me;
I am feeble in heart, but with you there is help;
I am restless but with you there is peace.

—Dietrick Bonhoeffer, used as a rosary prayer in Goulart, *God Has No Religion*

The Broken Prayer Beads

Toward the end of my two-year program in spiritual direction, one of my classmates made prayer beads for everyone. She is Episcopalian and made them in the Anglican tradition. Anglican prayer beads are comprised of four groups of seven beads called "weeks," divided by four cruciform beads. The "weeks" are meant to remind us of the days of creation, the temporal week, the seasons of the church year and the seven sacraments. The cruciform beads point to the cross as the central symbol of salvation, as well as the four seasons of the temporal year and the four points on a compass. The crosses most popularly used on the beads are the Celtic Cross and the Cross of San Damiano, which is said to have been the cross that Francis of Assisi prayed before when he believed God called him to rebuild the Church.

After class we were invited to choose a set of beads that we liked most. As I gazed on the various beads, I was interested in the earth-toned set with dark brown and gray stones and a Celtic Cross. I lifted them into my hand and felt the cool smoothness of the stones. That was the set I chose.

The word "bead" comes from an Old English word for "prayer." Beads and prayer have been synonymous over the decades. Having been raised Roman Catholic, I grew up with the rosary as a central part of our religious life. I am especially mindful of the times I exited the confessional booth after my "act of contrition" and, being absolved from my sins, sat in the quiet of the sanctuary praying the rosary.

I remember watching my grandmother pray the rosary during church and how quickly her fingers passed over each bead as she recited the Hail Mary and the Lord's Prayer at the specified intervals. I remember these beads wrapped around her hands as she lay in her coffin before we closed her away from the living world. I still have a pair of mother-of-pearl rosaries that were hers, in a small green floral box by my bedside.

The hand-made Anglican beads I chose that day at class have changed my way of using repetitive or centering prayer. They've also given me a new way of thinking about the rosary—less of a disciplinary tool and more of a meditative, calming one. I slip the beads into my pocket each morning as I head out to work. Throughout the day I can feel them against my leg, or I put my hand into my pocket and know that I am not tied to a desk or a phone or a computer but remain very much a part of the spiritual life.

The author Thomas Moore wrote in his book, *Care of the Soul,* that work is not set apart from the sacred. Often in monasteries work is as much a part of the monk's carefully designed life as prayer, meditation, and liturgy.[1]

I sometimes assign each of the cruciform beads the name of someone I want to remember in prayer throughout the day: a friend dealing with difficulties, another with cancer, my ninety-two-year-old aunt who wonders why she is still alive. On each of the little "weeks" beads I pray a revised version of the ancient Jesus Prayer ("have mercy on me") as a meditative way to calm my mind and let go of any stress or worry I might be feeling.

This Celtic set of prayer beads had become very dear to me until one day when I returned home from work, took them out of my pocket, and found the thread that bound them had broken. It was now in many little pieces. I was very annoyed as I searched

1. Moore, *Care of the Soul*, 180.

my pocket for all the round stone pieces. I put them into a glass bowl on my dresser and ruminated about their destruction. I went several weeks without the beads. Much of the time I forgot about them, but occasionally as I pulled open my dresser drawer looking for socks, I spied them still in the bowl. I knew that the longer they sat in that bowl, the greater my frustration would be for not repairing them. Those beads hounded me day after day until I eventually took the time to restring them.

Fine detailed work has never been my forte. My grandmother and mother both worked sorting buttons in a button factory during World War II days. I would rather have pushed a broom or driven a truck—anything but sorting buttons. So here I was sorting little stone beads, trying to put them back into the symmetric form they once had. After working my way through for about an hour, I finally finished. As I held the set of beads up, much to my dismay, they now hung cockeyed.

Once again I started up my daily regimen of putting the beads in my pocket each morning and using them throughout the day. I find they are even more meaningful now that I have restrung them. I like to think they are a metaphor for my spiritual life. When I start to take things for granted, or when I let my work get out of hand, things often fall apart. Sometimes all I need to do is take a little break, stop to rest, to listen, and to reach into my pocket and take out the prayer beads that remind me to greet even the cockeyed spiritual moments with thanksgiving.

UNTIL THE LAST BIRD SLEEPS

This day is done, and I am home.
I go and sit on the front porch.
It is a place of wisdom, and
a time for resting and waiting.
Sycamore branches bend to and fro
in the evening breeze.
Wind chimes tone various pitches
on the eaves just below where the
mother finch nests.
I tell myself I will sit here until
the last bird goes to sleep,
until there are no more chirps and
fluttering or winging back and forth
from tree to bush to tree.
I sit until there is no more
fretting over the last few seeds in the
feeder and the last ruckus of wings
in the water of the bird bath lay still.
And like the gusts of warm summer wind
that suddenly stop in the evening dusk,
the last bird tucks her small soft head
inside her wing and gently falls to sleep.

Tooter, Tooter! Remember to always be what you is and not what you is not. For people who is, are the happiest lot!

—Mr. Wizard the Lizard, in television show *Tooter Turtle*

Be What You Is

Tooter the Turtle always wanted to be someone special, someone supreme! He had aspirations of living the exciting life of a cowboy on the wide-open range. He could see himself sitting high on his pony and, with other cowboys, herding hundreds of mooing cattle. Tooter would anxiously go to see the magical Mr. Wizard the Lizard who lived in the crook of a big oak tree. Being way too big to fit through the little door, Tooter would call out, "Mr. Wizard, let me in!" A spell would be cast and Tooter would shrink to a size just right to fit into Mr. Wizard's tree house.

Once there, Tooter would share his aspirations with Mr. Wizard and ask if he would turn him into a cowboy. Always reluctant, Mr. Wizard would fulfill Tooter's wish. But the little turtle's fantasy would soon turn frantic. Being a cowboy was harder than he'd imagined. His herd of cattle would suddenly begin to stampede and he would find himself barely able to hang on to the saddle in the midst of galloping hoofs and flying dust. He would frantically cry out, "Help me, Mr. Wizard! I want to come home!" The wizard would wave his magic wand and in a strange little accent, call out an incantation: "Drizzle, drazzle, druzzle, drome; time for zis one to come home."

Tooter would stand there, exhausted and relieved. Mr. Wizard would give him repeated advice: "Be just vhat you is, not vhat you is not. Folks vhat is are ze happiest lot." Tooter never learned his lesson and frequently returned to the wizard in hopes of finding other exciting vocations.

You might remember this children's cartoon from the sixties. I had a fondness for Tooter and Mr. Wizard. And because I still think of these characters all these years later, I wonder if they have something more profound to say.

"Be what you is! Not what you is not!"

Many wise people have said this very same thing. Without going into the details of the existential theories of Kierkegaard and Nietzsche, an individual is solely responsible for giving his or her own life meaning and for living that life passionately and sincerely in spite of obstacles and distractions, including despair, angst, absurdity, alienation, and boredom. Mr. Wizard said all that, and much more, yet simply.

Sometimes I think we imagine God is like a Mr. Wizard; someone who is magically available to us and can get us away from obstacles, despair, distractions, and even the boredom that life often drapes over us. This is the God of fairy tales where wishes come true and there's always a happy ending.

The apostle Paul says in 1 Corinthians 13, "When I was a child, I talked like a child, I thought like a child, I reasoned like a child. When I became a man, I put childish ways behind me. Now we see but a poor reflection as in a mirror, then we shall see face to face."[1] And: "We'll see it all then, see it all as clearly as God sees us . . . "[2]

Are you being "just vhat you is"? Or trying to be "vhat you is not"? Perhaps each of us has a little Tooter inside—that cast-your-fate-to-the-wind thinker, wanting to be a cowboy. And I would not dismiss that being a cowboy, or cowgirl, might be a perfectly reasonable career for some of us.

Joseph Campbell told us to "follow your bliss." Even if we have left our childhood thinking behind, it doesn't mean we cannot see the very best of who we are at this moment and imagine what we could become in the next moment.

And God always says: Be what YOU is!

1. 1 Cor 13:11–12a (NIV).
2. 1 Cor 13:12b (MSG).

THE FECUNDITY OF GOD

(A Strawberry Island Poem)

Are you being motivated by love or fear?
Do you please, perform or pretend to be who
you need to be or rather who you are?
God in all Her fecundating spreads you out
like a great feast in the garden of eternity.
Spring forth with all your beauty, all your
pure knowledge, and be who you are meant to be.
Let your singing come forth;
Let your dancing be seen;
Let your music be heard;
Let your words ring out their truths;
Let your hands heal the earth;
Let your talents be tasted;
Let your heart open wide and nourish the Soul.
You are the fruit of your Mother's womb;
intellectually productive, inventive to a marked degree.
You are the great holy gift of God's fecundity.

Therefore I tell you, do not worry about your life, what you will eat or drink; or about your body, what you will wear. Is not life more important than food, and body more important than clothes? Look at the birds of the air; they do not sow or reap or store away in barns . . . See how the lilies of the field grow. They do not labor or spin.

—Matt 6:25–26a, 28a (NIV)

From Hot to Lukewarm

I have a relationship with time that is sometimes good and sometimes a source of anxiety. I am rather obsessed with knowing exactly how much time I need to do something or go somewhere so that I can accomplish whatever my task is in a timely manner. Because my relationship with time can become a task, I make sure to put on my watch just before I leave for work in the morning, and remove it as soon as I arrive home at night. I often do not wear my watch over the weekend so as to give my psyche a rest.

I've also developed a few ways to keep track of time without looking at my watch. I know that if I say twelve Jesus Prayers ("Lord have mercy on me") that approximately one minute will have gone by. This technique is especially helpful during spiritual direction or during a worship service when I want to give people some quiet time or centering time. The idea is to savor the time and create a kind of quietness which allows for the centering of my own self as well as others.

One technique I'm particularly fond of for tracking time has to do with the degree of heat in my morning coffee. From the time I pour the hot dark liquid into my cup to the time it becomes lukewarm is about ten minutes. This may vary depending on where I drink my coffee. If I'm reading the morning newspaper at the dining room table I can usually get through the two sections in about fifteen minutes before the coffee gets cold. Or sometimes I can do the Jumble Puzzle, but the Sudoku takes me far too long!

My favorite way to track time like this is on a Saturday morning when the clock does not stifle my schedule. My routine is to start a pot of coffee, then go out to the back deck to refill the bird feeders. I make sure to scatter some sunflower seeds along the wooden rail and lay out a few shelled peanuts for the blue jays, chickadees, and a few very familiar squirrels.

By the time my chore is complete, the coffee is done. I fix it just the way I like it and sit down in the old yellow-webbed rocker by the back screen door to observe the creatures without being a distraction. A flock of brown and gray feathers immediately gathers at the top of the mock orange waiting for the right moment to descend upon the feeders. I love the sound their wings make as they flutter back and forth. Having seed along the railing allows the opportunity for the fledglings to grab a morsel without the competition of their older and more aggressive mates. In the distance I can hear the blue jay announce his arrival and within minutes he soars in like a dart, grabs a nut, and swoops to the highest point of a maple tree.

If it's a very cold morning I might see the steam rise from the rim of my cup and feel the warmth around my fingers. Perhaps in the time that is passing, going from hot to lukewarm, I've had moments to chat with my grandfather whose memory is imprinted deep in my desire to be outside near the garden and the earth in all seasons. Or perhaps I've chatted a while with God, grateful for "what a beautiful morning it is" and wondering "how do you keep track of all that's happening?" In reality, I'm the one who's keeping track, not God.

In about ten minutes my coffee goes from hot to lukewarm. I've made time to care for these creatures and enjoy their presence. I've pushed away my own worries about what has to be done today or how much time I have in this day to do all the things I *should* be doing. I've learned that God doesn't really count minutes and doesn't require much more from me than a few moments of my time. And that I need to remember "do not worry about your life," and to trust all things to God.

ST. FRANCIS

Francis sits at the edge of the meadow
as the sky looms with thick and thunderous clouds.
A wind whispers "*Yahweh . . . Yahweh . . .* "
But he does not move nor does he flinch
when jagged lights bolt across the sky
and set the small bush burning like it did
eons ago for his brother Moses.
Moses always knew what to do.
Moses could hear the voice in the fire
and see the face of God in its flame.
Moses would do as he was told.
Francis sits holding a lamb in his lap,
protecting it from the wind and now
from the rain that pours in torrents.
Francis does not see God in the flame
that will not burn much longer.
As the storm passes, the flame dies.
The thin branches, now black and brittle,
are blown away in the aftermath.
The lamb climbs off Francis's lap, shakes away
the droplets of water, bleats a short wail,
and meanders back to the waiting flock huddled in the distance.
Francis sits at the edge of the meadow as the sun breaks out
from behind the parting clouds and waits for his clothes to dry.

Awareness is the space in which thoughts exist when that space has become conscious of itself.

—ECKHART TOLLE, *A NEW EARTH*

Squirrel Meditation

PEOPLE MEDITATE AT ALL hours of the day for all kinds of reasons. You may know the concept of centering meditation. It's a practice done to clear out the mind and calm the body before going into a longer period of meditation. Centering meditation is sometimes called centering prayer, and will often be done before starting spiritual direction or other religious gatherings.

I found on the internet, through YouTube, an endless array of meditation practice videos with a variety of teachers and platforms. There's Zen meditation, Christian meditation, Chakra meditation, Tibetan Buddhist meditation, Yoga meditation, healing meditation, and tons more. A good beginner's book that I've used and have recommended is Jack Kornfield's *Meditation for Beginners*. As Kornfield says in his first chapter, "When we take time to quiet ourselves we can all sense that our lives could be lived with greater compassion, and greater wakefulness."[1]

It is in this spirit that I began the art of what I call "squirrel meditation."

I didn't intend for squirrels to be an intricate part of my daily meditation, though I've always been mindful of their existence in and around our neighborhood. Just about anywhere I went throughout the day, there they were! And I didn't intend to become intentionally drawn to a select few neighborhood squirrels,

1. Kornfield, *Meditation for Beginners*, 2.

that have, in particular, taught me some unique methods in meditating, but I have. It all started with Scarface.

One winter morning I looked out on the back deck and a gray squirrel was sitting there with a scarred-up face as though it had been bitten or injured in an accident. I took compassion on it and put out a box with a blanket and some food. The squirrel never used the box, but it did eat the food. As the months moved into spring, Scarface came to visit each morning looking for the peanuts that I put out on the back deck.

When the weather became warm, I sat in my old webbed rocking chair and drank my morning coffee while Scarface ate peanuts. At first I thought about the squirrel's life, how it became injured, where it lived. But as the days went on, I found myself just sitting there quietly enjoying the space between us, and I began to think about my life. I never considered our quiet time together a form of mediation. But I observed that when I came back into the house I was calm and serene, feeling much like I do when I meditate.

An article in *Presence Magazine: An International Journal of Spiritual Direction* focuses on animals and prayer. The writer states that slowing down enough to see where and what the Holy is calling us to is itself a form of prayer. She further goes on to say how observing animals can teach us to pause and reflect on their ability to *be* and not to *do*.[2] These were two verbs that I began to share with my squirrel-mate.

During a Lenten study group at my church, we read the book *The Wisdom Jesus* by Cynthia Bourgeault. One of the chapters that was most interesting to me was "Centering Prayer Meditation." Bourgeault says that centering prayer is not all about kenosis, or emptying one's mind or self, but rather that "it goes *straight for the heart* (emphasis added)."[3] It is a gentle way to let go of the busyness in our minds and center our thinking in matters of the heart. Sometimes a sacred word or two is used along with the breath, like "breathing in, I am peaceful; breathing out, I am well."

2. Chernoff, "Animals," 39.

3. Bourgeault, *Wisdom Jesus*, 142.

I imagine little Scarface as "breathing in, peanut good; breathing out, peanut very good," then turning to me with the incantation of "more peanuts . . . more peanuts . . . more peanuts." And I, having developed a keener sense of wakefulness and compassion, gently rise and go get more peanuts.

BLESSED BY A DRAGONFLY

(A Strawberry Island Poem)

Days have come and gone
and I have learned to tread
the place I walk lightly and
know the ground, air and water
are homes for other living things.
I am painted with a sacred
coating of serenity; images of
red and gold linger in my
thoughts much like the sun that sets
and paints the water in shimmering glints
resembling the colors of heaven,
so I am told by the passing of a
dragonfly, its rainbow wings
coupled and ever twittering,
fanning the moist afternoon air;
humming, dancing, darting about
my forehead, placing a kiss there;
implanting a secret that took
her whole life to know.
As I recover from her prayer,
she tells me it is time to go.
I am charged with holding tight
this covenant which coats my skin,
so as not to let the ways of
the world find their antagonisms
through my weaknesses, blocking out the

education of this moment;
and in this sacred journey I take
keep the blessing of the dragonfly
within.

According to one ancient Egyptian myth, honey bees were the tears of the sun god Ra. In this context, the bee was seen as the messenger of the gods, falling down, like tears, towards the earth . . . to pass on some secret message.

—Eugenia Di Guglielmo, website of the European School Education Platform

The Mystery of Wasps

I used to travel to Strawberry Island in Canada for silent retreats. I took a boat to a small island that was not more than a mile in diameter, and I had the most extraordinary experiences.

Strawberry Island sits in the middle of Lake Simcoe, north of Toronto. According to Basilian Father E.J. LaJeunesse, it was Indian land until 1856 when the government obtained a title to it. For many years, the island was a popular summer resort. In 1922, the religious order of the Basilian Fathers bought the island. They arrived to find it overrun with bats! The little black squatters had taken up residence in an old hotel and it took a few years to vanquish the prolific nocturnal creatures. The Basilian community named their first means of transportation to the island—a temperamental and leaky old launch—"The Bat." For the past eighty years until recently, Strawberry Island was a spiritual retreat center run by the Toronto-based Basilian Brothers. Pope John Paul II was the island's most famous visitor and stayed for a few days in 2002 during his visit to Toronto's World Youth Day.

One of my extraordinary experiences occurred on a warm summer afternoon following mass in the chapel. I began a mindful walk through the woods on the island. Mindful walking entails purposeful steps, observing your surroundings, and listening to and feeling the earth beneath your feet. Finding sacred places on the island was an easy task, as they were everywhere. Paths wound through the woods and along the edge of the slopes that overlooked the lake. The sun slipped through the branches and danced over the thick foliage that seemed to breath with me as I walked.

At one point I came across a stone grotto that housed a statue of Mary. In front of the statue was a large stone table that resembled an altar. About six feet out from the grotto was a wooden bench. I sat down and felt prayerful in the moment. Sometimes God is perfectly content with us just being present; no words, no petitions, no worries or plans to be made. I sat in silence for about ten minutes and then I had the desire to go to the altar and be closer to the statue of Mary.

I stood up and began to walk forward, then stopped. Swarming all around the underside of the stone table were wasps. They darted up and around the smooth stone top and I could hear the hum of their wings. I noticed the small cone hive hanging in the corner of one of the legs. I slowly backed away and sat down again, thinking I could not approach. I was fearful of the wasps attacking me. It would be different if there were just one or two, but there was a swarm of about twenty of them.

I sat very still and continued being prayerful, taking in the sound of the buzzing, the darting movements, the wind in the leaves of the trees, and the wild vegetation that surrounded the grotto. I was continually plagued by an inner voice that called me to come to the altar, but I didn't want to go any closer; I wanted to remain at a safe distance. How often do we make these decisions to stay away from what scares us, what seems fearful, and to stay where we think it is safe?

As I sat still and was torn between the calling and the staying, I began to talk to Mary. I said, "I cannot come close right now."

And she asked, "Why?"

And I said, "I am afraid of the wasps."

And she answered, "Don't be afraid of them . . . come and see me."

After a few moments I gathered my courage and stood up and walked slowly to the table. I kept my eyes fixed on the statue in the grotto and not on the stone table. When I was about a foot away, I looked down, and there was not a wasp to be found. They were gone.

I cannot find a logical reason for this experience. I only know that when I was called to come forward, I had a desire to do so and my fear went away. When I got to the table the face of Mary was gentle and kind and I stood for several minutes, with tears of wonder, relief, and gratitude. Whether it was a gift from the Holy or just a mystery of wasps, I'll never know. I turned away to continue my mindful walking and would remember this moment for years to come.

VISIONS OF THE VIRGIN

Is this your mother, little boy?
A child, yet herself
clinging to the arm of
a tender old man.
Blessed with bewilderment
is She;
the message of an Angel:
"Sacred are you among women,
and holy is the fruit of your womb."
But children grow up
He is no longer a little boy,
nor She still a virgin.
Yes,
She is
full of Grace,
beloved,
wild and
beautiful;
everlasting in
the folklore of humanity,
and never ever
just a Mother.

That master weaver, whose skills are beyond
our knowing, has stretched his warp through the world.
He has fastened his loom between earth and sky,
where the shuttlecocks are the sun and the moon.

—Kabir, in *Songs of the Saints of India*

The Coin, the Bible, and the Hindu Temple

I once joined an interfaith group called the Christian Hindu Dialogue, in which about five Christians and five Hindus gathered once a month to discuss religious tradition and to seek commonality and understanding from each other's religious tradition. I think that out of all the religions I have come to know over my many years, Hinduism feels the most familiar to me. It is the world's oldest religion, the largest non-biblical tradition, and it sees its origin in the cosmic mind itself.

A few weeks after I first began meeting with the group, we had an engaging conversation about karma and reincarnation. Vaishnava Shakti is the force that stuns the soul at the time of rebirth so that it loses conscious memory of its past life. The Karmashaya is the karmic residue we carry from past lives, our old memories and habits and desires, which are stored in our subtle body—an energetic dimension that exists beyond our physical body. It's our karmic DNA.[1]

There are three kinds of Karma:

Sanchita—all the karma accrued during previous lives;

1. Johnsen, *Hinduism*, 96.

Prarabdha—the portion of karma destined to play out in the present life;

Kriyamana—the new karma being produced in the current incarnation.

I want to share my thoughts about Kriyamana.

After the meeting where we discussed karma, I removed my shoes in the coat room, and climbed a long staircase and entered the temple. Some members were finishing evening prayers. I love the sounds and music of Hindu rituals. The room I was in was expansive and filled with many manifestations of God, smells of incense, and gifts of fruits and nuts. In my Christian place of worship, the sanctuary has many stained glassed windows, and long gothic lamps hang from the high ceiling. In worship, we are mostly on "the same page" of ritual or traditional liturgy. In the Hindu tradition, each person is with God separately, having their own personal experience. *The Bhagavad Gita* states, "In the still mind, the depths of mediation, the Self reveals itself. Beholding the Self, by means of the Self, an aspirant knows the joy and peace of complete fulfillment."[2]

I stayed for a while after the prayer service, sitting quietly in the temple. Most everyone had left, except the priest who was extinguishing candles and preparing to close the room. I left and returned to the coat room for my shoes. I gathered my belongings and started out the door when I saw on the floor several coins that looked like foreign money. I did not know where they had come from nor did I know their value. I picked them up and put them in my pocket and went home. When I got home I realized I had left my Bible on the table in our discussion room. The next morning I called the temple and they said the priest had found it and was keeping it safe for me. I said I would pick it up later in the afternoon.

After work I drove back to the temple, which sits far off a country road and is surrounded by green fields and trees. Only one other car was in the parking lot. I entered the building, left

2. *Bhagavad Gita* 6:20.

my shoes in the coatroom, and climbed the stairs to the temple. In the front of the room by the large statue of Vishnu (preserver of the world and saver of the dharma), was the head priest dressed in a bright orange wrap called a lungi. He saw me and waved me forward. "You are here for your Bible?" he asked. "Yes . . . thank you for keeping it," I replied.

He went behind a floor-to-ceiling curtain and returned with my Bible and a banana. He said it was a gift from the gods. I thanked him, we bowed and I left. As I returned to the coatroom, I put my hand into my coat pocket and felt the coins I had found the night before. On the floor by the door were the priest's shoes. I took the coins and put them into his right shoe and then left the temple.

I cannot say if this experience reflected any karma or if the experience over those twenty-four hours even mattered one way or another. I do know that in my heart I felt a pleasant goodness.

ON BEING ALL ONE

If we see with Christ eyes
then we will know what is true;
If we listen with Christ ears
then we will hear the sounds of Love;
If we love with a Christ heart
then our love will be pure;
And with our arms open wide
we will greet one another in peace
and in the knowledge we are
all one of the same Body.

A worker, wed to purpose and things,
Earth-worn I turn from day's sufficiency.
One lethed hour that duty never brings,
Oh! one dim hour to drift, Moth Moon, with thee!

—FLORENCE RIPLEY MASTIN, "MOTH MOON"

The Moth and the Moon

I WALKED ACROSS THE hallway one night and looked into my study to find our gray cat, Smoke, watching something on the ceiling. I looked up to see a small moth circling the ivory globe light fixture. It looked like a moth circling the moon. I watched the two of them for a few minutes, wondering if the cat would bring the moth to a quick demise. But Smoke tired of the game and walked away. A little while later I returned to shut off the light and we all went to bed.

Dusk came early to the sky as I returned from work the next day. October was wet and damp and becoming very stingy with daylight. After a quick meal for me and the cats (there are four all total and that's another story), I returned to my study. I flicked on the globe ceiling light and another of our cats, Sophie, looked up with glee at the sudden burst of fluttering around the moon lamp. The moth was still alive.

This time I sat down and watched for a while. Sophie and I both anchored our heads back, eyes toward the ceiling, and watched the moth circle and bounce off the light. It had endless energy. I wondered where it slept all night and day. Does it know there are cats in the house that would enjoy a playful pounce upon its soft dusty frame? Sophie watched very carefully as the moth zipped up and down and round in a mad frenzy.

I began to wonder if this wasn't some past soul, an incarnation of someone who once knew me. Who could it be? Who would come back as a moth? Do people come back as insects? I've heard of reincarnation of souls as other humans, animals, or maybe trees, so I guess a moth is plausible. Now I know that a moth can live more than a day, so it's better to be a moth than a fly. Thinking of my relatives, there isn't a one that I would consider moth-like. But then, what are moths like?

After an extensive search through Google, I found the right photo to match my moth. (Already I am laying down ownership.) To the best of my knowledge, and I viewed at least one hundred moth photos, it is a grass-veneer moth. It was born sometime in June and is expected to live through October. It was once a larva that probably hung out in the grass until it morphed into its sleek slender self. I would guess it fed on leaves, as I don't think moths are carnivorous. But then, I haven't really studied moths before. I was quickly becoming attached to this one.

As I surfed the Internet, the moth landed on my computer terminal and seemed to enjoy viewing the many varieties of itself. Occasionally I asked if it knew this one or that one. And a few times we both lingered over the more decorative wings of the "movie star moths" in their ostentatious splendor.

Now that I've researched the little guy, I'm more certain than ever he has intentionally come to be my companion through the last few days of his life. Maybe it's a female, but somehow I can't imagine any of my female friends or family members coming back as a moth. It must be a guy moth. You know the ones who circle around and around and around because they don't want to ask directions! Or the ones who slam over and over and over into a window pane trying to get to a light inside another room. Or the ones who flitter around a flame until they get too close, and "poof" they're gone.

This is a brave and clever little moth. Sophie has not grown tired of watching it spring from the terminal screen back up to the moon lamp, and then very foolishly over to the balcony door. Sophie makes her move. The moth lies still and motionless as Sophie reaches out her paw, gently and quickly, giving the little guy a push. He lifts and circles above the furry head as if teasing her. "Catch me if you can!" Sophie strikes and misses. The moth flies up and then dives at her.

She is stunned. Again she strikes with her gray, clawless front paw. Again she misses, and the lucky little moth heads back to the light of the moon. I'm not sure how long this risky behavior will allow us time together in these last days.

As I finish my thoughts, the room is quiet. Sophie has gone to rest on her favorite chair, most certainly exhausted from her safari. I finish these last few words and wonder still about who has come back to entertain me. Could this be Uncle Dominic? He was a fine companion to me as a child. He had white hair, was only about five feet tall, and had a magnificent Italian accent. I do believe Dominic is a fine name for a Grass-Veneer Moth.

CALLED TO THE WILDNESS OF GOD

(A Strawberry Island poem)

Surely the wildness of God has
come to play with us.
Can you remember when you
were wild for play? When you didn't
want to stop for nothing, not supper,
not resting and certainly not sleeping.
On this first day I am called once again
to lay gentle and quiet in this wildness;
I am called by the bell to come and eat,
made to stop and sit in restful silence.
Called to be quiet and mindful of my ways,
My walk, my talk, my thinking, my breathing.
Consider the spiders, they do not worry or
fret about what they will eat or where they
will go in this warm early morning.
They do not tarry, but build their tenuous
webs over and over again as we foolish
beings walk through them every time we
step out into the wildness of God.

For every house is built by someone, but
God is the builder of everything.

—HEB 3:4 (NIV)

Down Comes a Home

I STOOD FOR ABOUT an hour and watched the house next to the church where I work get torn down by a backhoe. The small man and the moving machine with a head like a dinosaur took about half a day to tear down what probably took people at the least, a few weeks to build at the turn of the twentieth century. Years, this house stood, through changes in owners, in the neighborhood, in society. It stood through two world wars and then some, scores of storms and blizzards, and even months of vacancy and an attempt at vandalism and torching.

Now I look out my office window and where there once stood a large house with a roof and brick chimney, gables and windows, gutters and porch steps, there is a pile of stones and rubble. At one point during the demolition someone commented that the backhoe looked like a dinosaur eating corn. "Chomp, chomp, chomp!" The roof was gone.

In 1 Kings you will read that Solomon built a magnificent temple from limestone and cedar wood, using the best materials available at the time, and it took over seven years.[1] It was destroyed in a far shorter time by the Romans in 70 CE during the Siege of Jerusalem.

It took only two large dumpster truck fills to haul away the broken-up house. Out came doors and walls. A hot water tank dangled high up on conduit wire, then tumbled to the pile of

1. 1 Kgs 6:7–38 (NIV).

bricks and wood below. Sections of floor came crunching out like crinkled wax paper magnified in sound one hundred times greater.

I wondered about the people who first lived in the house. Were they invisibly standing around with the rest of us watching the walls of their home fall? And what of the people in Jerusalem? Was it not a heartsick moment for all? So precise was the mouth of this hoe. It seemed to bite down, then pull back, then push forward, compacting the walls into sawdust and sticks. In two days, it was over. The garage that was only seven feet from my window was the last thing to go.

It is said that we should not build up temples and material goods for ourselves in this world. They will eventually waste away by storms, sieges, and the passing of time. Our sanctuaries are holy. We find peace and tranquility in them, whether churches or houses. "For every house is built by someone." And God will be the builder, and we shall thoughtfully pause before taking it down.

INSIDE YOUR SELF

Save yourself little Soul;
Pull the Holy Light up
over your heart and
know you are complete
and perfect;
There is nowhere you
can hide from the
Sacred Sound of Love.
It will permeate your being;
It will circle and surround
you like your breathing.
You are not lost—
you are found.

. . . you will find [God] if you look . . . with all your heart . . .

—Deut 4:29 (NIV)

Walking a Labyrinth

I have walked many labyrinths in my life, and have always been drawn to this ancient spiritual mystery. My favorite labyrinths have been outdoors: in the forest, like the one I've walked the most in the Adirondacks at the old Priory Retreat House, and the labyrinth at the edge of Long Island Sound at Mercy by the Sea Monastery. I've walked indoor labyrinths, too: once at the 213th General Assembly of the Presbyterian Church USA in Louisville, Kentucky, and at least once a year during the season of Lent, the labyrinth at Asbury United Methodist Church in Rochester, New York.

There are some who have journeyed to far-off places to walk ancient labyrinths, like the most familiar Chartres Cathedral labyrinth in France. I'm not sure I will ever get to walk a labyrinth quite as elaborate and ancient as that, but even the simple ones we build in our personal sacred spaces are places of holy good, echoing those that date back 4,000 years. Whether we are in France or in our home town, walking the labyrinth will lead us to our spiritual center.

I can't say I remember walking my very first labyrinth, but I did have one experience that is very memorable. During Lent, I invited members of my home church to join me at Asbury for a sacred walk. We met at four o'clock in the lower fellowship hall. A beautiful marble labyrinth was etched into the floor and there were strands of small white lights circling the area. A harpist had come to play meditative music, which added to the ambience in the room.

We removed our shoes and each took a turn entering the sacred space. There was a basket of smooth stones for those who wished to take one on the walk, and a small brass gong to strike upon entering and exiting. I brought a variety of scripture passages and quotes from poems on scraps of paper to share, as sometimes newcomers don't know what to do while they walk. This would help center them. I was hoping it would be a meaningful and spiritual experience.

The labyrinth, for me, is a metaphor for life. It is like being on a path that we know will soon lead to the center. As we walk, we will make turns that seem to be going back to where we started, but as we continue, we are actually moving forward. We will come across others walking the labyrinth. Sometimes we will walk alongside people and sometimes they will be in front of us or behind us. We may have to go around them or they may have to go around us.

The first few minutes of our prayerful walk that day were genuinely lovely. I saw some people reading from the scraps of paper, and others holding their smooth stones. A kind of peacefulness had settled in the room. The music from the harp gently spun through the room like harmony with the movements we took passing one another, stopping now and then to read or pray or just be still.

Suddenly the door to the room swung open and a woman walked in wearing jogging pants, sneakers, and a pedometer on her wrist. She quickly moved to the beginning of the labyrinth, hit the gong, and started what seemed to me to be a power walk. I tried to remain focused and non-judgmental. Then two other women, who looked to be in their eighties, entered the room. They admitted to never having been on a labyrinth, and just stepped on at random spots and began walking around, mostly following the paths, but sometimes crossing over. It was rather like a dream in which you are observing a somewhat chaotic moment in time.

I was relieved when I reached the end of my walk. I stepped off, tapped the gong, and sat down to watch from the sidelines the rest of what seemed a very peculiar race. At first, I was perturbed. Why wasn't there someone facilitating this labyrinth? As someone who worked for an agency where I was mostly in charge, my authoritative "self" struggled to resist wanting to fix things. Then

I heard a voice inside my head say, "But isn't this what life is all about? You cannot control the experience of the holy."

One by one the members of my church stepped off the labyrinth. As our eyes met, I saw they were all smiling.

LIFE IN A LABYRINTH

I stand at the start of this
labyrinth and breathe the musty air
in the dim room before beginning the journey.
The first few steps seem awkward
but then a simple rhythm pulls me
forward—one step then another.
Should I pray?
Should I discern the fact I do not
know where this path is going?
I walk and stop occasionally and
look up to see who is walking with me.
And there you are, walking toward me.
You seem deep in thought.
Or maybe you are just thinking about
the moment you opened your eyes
this morning and knew there was
another day to be lived.
Like me, you take one step and then another.
I am on the far outside of the path
and you are entering the center.
Somewhere along the way we cross.
My hand touches yours and in one small
moment the Soul has a memory:
"I remember you."
Now you are walking the edge
and I am entering the center.

Promise me you'll remember—You're braver than you believe, and stronger than you seem, and smarter than you think.

—ATTRIBUTED TO CHRISTOPHER ROBIN, SPEAKING TO WINNIE THE POOH

In Place of Terror

HOW DID THE WORLD get to be so violent? Was it always this way and maybe I was too naïve to notice? Was I too busy and too self-absorbed to see humanity erupting into a hurricane of discontent and anger? Certainly not all of us are angry and discontented. I am not usually an angry or discontented person, and I'm certainly not violent. But I find my disposition is often tested.

When the large black ants invaded my kitchen that spring morning, I began to think violent thoughts. The creeping invasive warriors congregated in the butter mint bowl. Oh horrors! They were swarming and rolling all over the yellow bits of candy, feasting on their sugary treasure. Without a moment's hesitation I washed it all down the drain with hot sudsy water.

It was a spontaneous move on my part. I didn't want the insects to take over the kitchen. It needed to be done and I was the one to do it.

My spouse Peg is a pacifist. She would rather I had patiently taken the bowl of mints outside and let the black ants escape into the earth where they belong. She would willingly go out of her way to save the smaller species. Which leads me into a related story.

We were staying one summer at a bed and breakfast on Cayuga Lake in the Finger Lakes region of New York. The evening settled in and Peg read to me from a novel. Reading to one another is something we have done for many years. As her voice continued,

I happened to notice something dark moving across the ceiling by the sliding glass doors. At first, I thought it was a small bat. I interrupted Peg and asked what she thought about it. We both surreptitiously crept closer to find it was a very fat wolf spider about the size of a baby's hand. I had never seen one this big. Peg said we must save it. At that moment I thought to myself that I am the one who needs to be saved, not the spider. And honestly, I haven't a clue as to how we will convince it to go outside. She says we will get a plastic bag and I will hold the bag while she taps the spider, which has now crawled over the top of the drape covering the glass door. "No" I say. *She* will hold the bag and I will tap the back of the drape in the hopes the humungous spider will fall or jump into it.

This has now become a prayerful moment. I must stand on a chair and maneuver myself to the back side of the insect that I'm sure is watching my every move. I am talking to St. Michael, patron saint of brave warriors. I can do this. Together we count to three and I swat the back of the drape with the book we were reading. The spider falls into the bag, Peg swiftly closes it, and she rushes outside to find a safe place where it can crawl out and continue terrorizing other guests.

I consider myself a pacifist to a point. But I am not a purist and oftentimes I am a coward. Peg is the pacifist in the truest sense. She will go out of her way to save anything, even me, if need be. Which, of course, she exemplified in this experience.

This is the way of the true warrior—the true pacifist. St. Michael was proud.

OHM WATCHING

Out on a limb,
broke in a small
wet place, I watch
a turtle bring herself
up through deep roots
to where some might
call Wisdom.
"Go this way,"
they said;
The wise ones,
the wicked ones,
the ones who
thought they held
the sacred Light.
They do not.
Only the turtle knew
the sound of ohm.
She kept it low and safe inside,
then breathed out when
it was ready to be heard.
They cannot breathe it.
When it was ready to
be seen, the sacred Light
poured from turtle's heart,
springing forth like holy
beams, free at last from
where it hid, on the tips of
each new rising moon.

Getting to know you,
Getting to know all about you. . . .
When I am with you,
Getting to know what to say.

—Oscar Hammerstein II, "Getting to Know You"

Can You See Me?

A while back I had the privilege of speaking at a friend's installation at a little white church in Morganville, NY, a perfect little town with a horse farm across the road from the church. Many people came to celebrate the occasion.

When it was my turn to speak, I made my way up to the pulpit and, as always, I stood a little on tip-toe, as I am short in height, just over five feet. I looked out at the congregation, smiled and said "Can everyone see me?" There were a few chuckles and smiles back at me from the congregation. I continued to share how I knew the pastor and I read a poem from Billy Collins, one of my favorite poets.

After about ten minutes I sat back down, very relieved that all went well. You see, I have some performance anxiety, and although I have always been in the public eye, so to speak, I have always preferred to stand back from an audience. People might think just the opposite of me as they see me in various public arenas, on the pulpit, on the opinion page of our newspaper, and especially now in social media, where I love to share my life experiences and "chat" with friends and family.

But "Can you see me?" I thought about this question that got the chuckle and began to hear a deeper question, with a deeper meaning. "Can you really see me?" Do you know who I am? Do any of us really know each other's sacred stories? There seems to be fear about sharing what's at our core self, and yet I think sometimes that is what is most important in "seeing" one another. It's when I tell my story that you can begin to really see me. And when you tell your story, I begin to really see you. I think sometimes that if more of us had this opportunity there wouldn't be so much anxiety, animosity, or misunderstandings. And perhaps there would not be so many lonely people in the world.

I think about some of the words from the Billy Collins poem I read that day, "Aimless Love," from his book, *Nine Horses*, and how they speak of ways to truly see one another:

> *This is the best kind of love, I thought,*
> *Without recompense, without gifts,*
> *Or unkind words, without suspicion,*
> *Or silence on the telephone.*[1]

1. Collins, *Nine Horses*, 17–18.

SONGBIRD

(A Strawberry Island Poem)

You, who sit in anonymity,
hidden in high branches that bend
with the wind, sing your sweet
composition, melodic and
enchanting, almost mesmerizing
as the music blends with the
dancing light over the lake,
patterns ever changing, moving
leaves and clouds, never resting,
like you, sweet winged bird,
constant in your concert, mixing
another chorus, voices that make
a perfect enchanted melody.
And I, with simple talents, take
the moment to stop and listen
to your joyful operetta.

Some of us think that holding on makes us strong, but sometimes it is letting go.

—Herman Hesse, *Siddartha*

The God Box

In my office there is an oval table on which I have a small altar with the following items: a daily meditation booklet, a covered candle, a ceramic angel figure from my childhood, a postcard of an Orthodox drawing of Mary and Jesus, and a "God box." There's also a teapot and two small cups made in Hawaii along with my very first "congratulations on retiring" (soon!) card, but it's the God box I want to tell you about.

In Anne Lamott's book *HELP, THANKS, WOW: The Three Essential Prayers,* she writes: "One modest tool for letting go in prayer that I've used for twenty-five years is a God box . . . I write down the name of the person about whom I am so distressed or angry, or describe the situation that is killing me, with which I am so toxically, crazily obsessed, and I fold the note up, stick it in the box and close it. You might have a brief moment of prayer . . . "[1]

It has been my practice, each morning when I enter my office, to read a daily meditation and light a candle for people and situations I want to thoughtfully remember throughout the day. One situation in particular was haunting me. Unlike my other concerns, I felt I needed to do something to "fix it." There must be something I had done that I could undo.

After many months of distress about something over which I had no control, and which I lamented endlessly, even lamenting over my lamenting, I came across the chapter in Lamott's book

1. Lamott, *HELP, THANKS, WOW*, 36.

about the God box. I decided making a God box would be a way of putting the torment aside and giving to God the task of lamentation or whatever the "fix it" might be. The solution that might manifest could very well be something I didn't expect or want in a resolution. I had to trust the outcome, trust God.

I found an empty little tea canister, created a label that said "God box," penned my concern on a small piece of paper, folded it in fours, put it into the box, and closed the lid. Now it sits on the altar and each morning I light the candle and read the meditation and think about the people and things that are coming in and out of my life. The God box is like a covenant between me and God in which I assume there will be a successful miracle of sorts sometime before I die.

I must say I no longer lament. Occasionally a little catch comes to the throat and the eyes get moist, but it doesn't belong to me anymore. Like the fluff that comes off the Cottonwood trees every spring, I am amazed at how gently it passes by and disappears into the sky.

MOMENTS OF SURRENDER

(A Strawberry Island Poem)

Bats in the hallway,
baby birds under stairs,
spiders spin their silvery webs
that follow us everywhere;
mosquitoes at our beck and call,
deer flies eat our skin;
falling out of red canoes;
where did this all begin?
Butterflies along the gardens,
day lilies of orange and yellow;
glints of sunlight dance on the waves,
songs of red and blue barn swallows.
Walking up and down the steps,
sitting by the shore;
watching sunsets steeped in splendor;
to be loved and held in arms so tender;
oh, for this sweet moment of surrender,
and the knowledge we need nothing more.

The trouble is you never see anyone
sitting in these forlorn chairs
though at one time it must have seemed
a good place to stop and do nothing for a while.

—Billy Collins, "The Chairs That No One Sits In," *Aimless Love*

Upon the Sitting of a Pope

In 1958 Pope Pius XII died. In 1963 the beloved John XXIII died after only five years of leadership. Pope Paul VI was next and led for about fifteen years. This was the only pope I remember from my youth, and I remember him having a kind face. In 1978 John Paul I was appointed and died within a week. Then Pope John Paul II was appointed. I was still a practicing Catholic at that time, and very much steeped in Catholicism. I remember the whole world mourning as I watched the events unfold. The puff of white smoke from the Vatican announced a new pope had been elected—a poor Polish man who would lead the Church for nearly thirty years and become loved by millions.

I later left the Catholic Church but not its mystic essence. In Catholic tradition, the pope is a descendant of the Apostle Peter, of whom Jesus states, "on this rock I will build my church."[1]

There's a story I like to tell about Pope John Paul II. In 2002 I went on retreat at Strawberry Island on Lake Simcoe in Ontario, Canada—the quiet retreat center that I came to know through the local Sisters of St. Joseph. I traveled there once a year in July to take time off from the stress of work and to get my energy back. I was well fed, well cared for, and my soul was nourished.

1. Matt 16:18 (NIV).

That year held more excitement than ever on the island. The Pope was coming the following week for a brief rest before attending World Youth Day in Toronto. Our little bunkhouse was being overhauled to meet the Holy See's needs. There was a sense of disbelief about the fact that he would be staying in the same building in which we scurried about late at night in our pajamas. There was also a sense of awe about the fact that he would walk the same paths along the island, see the same trees and shrubs and the little minks that run out from the shore of the lake. He might stand at the edge of the shoreline and watch the sunset, just as we had made it our ritual to do together each night.

This was the Pope! It wasn't the president of some foreign country or a famous movie star. It was the descendant of Peter . . . maybe. There were mixed thoughts about this and about his coming. Many agreed he would get a much-needed rest in this place, and come to enjoy the island as we all had. Some of the younger sisters saw the Pope as an antiquated figurehead who kept the Church in the dark ages. Others saw him as a man of great mystery and reverence. Many of us had much respect and love for him.

John Paul II had gotten very frail in his old age and also with the onset of Parkinson's Disease, so a wooden ramp was constructed at the base of the bunkhouse where he would stay. Two lower bedrooms were converted into one suite with a very simple but modern shower and bathroom. The Pope's bedroom was in one room and his attendant's bedroom was in the other. We left the island that year with great anticipation of his visit.

The following year I returned once again to Strawberry Island for my annual retreat. I was assigned a room on the second floor of the bunkhouse. One day after I returned to the bunkhouse from my meditation walk, I strolled by the room where the Pope had stayed and found the door open. I walked in and looked around. It was a simple plain room with a full-size bed. There was contemporary furniture, and in the corner, a hard-back wooden chair with a red cushion. Was this where the Pope had sat? If I sat down, would I have some surreal experience? Would there be a miracle? Should I pray for one? I sat quietly. I had no vision and no extrasensory experience. I did, however, feel very privileged to sit in that chair. After a few minutes I stood up and silently thanked whoever left the door open, because when I came back later it was shut and locked.

I remember hearing that at that World Youth Day in Toronto, the Pope said it was especially up to the young people to take on the great task of building a society with more justice and solidarity.

John Paul II died on April 2, 2005. He was a much-loved man, and I considered him a great world mystic. Even though I no longer follow the traditions of the Roman Catholic Church, I am pleased to say that I was humbled to sit in the Pope's chair.

GRASS PATHS

(A Strawberry Island Poem)

Patterns on the ground,
laden green, shoots of
supple grass carpet the
lawn and trim each tree
and garden like a mote.
I walk and gaze upon the
streaks of trodden paths
before me, stems bent over
from passing shoes and
scuffing sandals, leading from
one place to the next, each step
taken falls upon those who
go before me—journey on;
Grass paths that lead to home
and grace and holy space that
starts even in the pace of those
who I do not see.
Patterns on the ground,
laden green;
brush strokes from passing
pilgrims' feet.

I will love the light for it shows me the way; yet I will love the darkness for it shows me the stars.

—Og Mandino, *The Greatest Salesman*

About the Light

Here in the Northeast I see the light returning from winter's hibernation. It has been a long and dark winter for many of us. It has been extremely cold and very snowy. I think back to when I was a kid and loved this kind of weather. In fact, weather in general never seemed to pose a problem. One just lived around it and through it. But the lack of light was another thing. The absence of the light was always profound in one way or another for me. I think of how we use the word:

light
to be light
to see light
to feel light
to light up
to be lit

There are a ton of references to light in the Bible. Some that are familiar, that I find visual and poetic:

> "And God said, 'Let there be light, and there was light.'"
> "And God said, 'Let there be lights in the [vault] of the sky to separate the day from the night, and let them serve as signs to mark seasons and days and years . . .'"
> ". . . like the light of morning at sunrise on a cloudless morning, like the brightness after rain that brings the grass from the earth."[1]

1. Gen 1:3, Gen 1:14, and 2 Sam 23:4 (NIV).

According to the Greek Orthodox mystic Gregory Palamas, there are three kinds of spiritual light: sensible light, intellectual light, and uncreated light. He believed that spiritual experiences influenced us not only spiritually but also physically. "For the uncreated energies are the energies of light and of love."[2] Augustine, John of the Cross, Hildegaard of Bingen, and Teresa of Avila all spoke of the light, not just of God, but within others—people that they knew in their lives—and moments they experienced. This light is in all that surrounds us if we have eyes to see, the heart to feel, and the mind to comprehend a reason for the light. Even in the mystery of it, there is reason for light, regardless of whether we understand it. Jesus said, "I am the light of the world. Whoever follows me will never walk in darkness, but will have the light of life."[3]

It is said that as the Buddha lay dying and his disciples sat around him, they were concerned and worried, wondering who would now be their teacher, their guiding light. Buddha answered that they must be their own light. Robert Welton, author of *Be Your Own Light*, says, "Everyone has their own light. Inside each of us is the glow of the memory of who we really are, where we come from, and where we are going. In this light, the sound of truth can be heard, clear as a temple bell."[4]

Og Mandino said he could love the darkness because he could better see the stars.[5] I can almost see the light at the end of the season of winter—the long tunnel of darkness. The spring equinox will come and the sun will once again spread its light over the white bark of the sycamore trees. Even when we close our eyes we can still see the light. In our darkest moments, when all else fails our senses, we must remember this light, and know that we will again be transformed by it.

2. Johnston, *Mystical Theology*, 60.
3. John 8:12 (NIV).
4. Welton, "Be Your Own Light," para. 4.
5. Mandino, *The Scroll Marked II*, 59.

THE HUG

(A Strawberry Island Poem)

Early evening sets this sun
in lavender and orange stripes
across the sky as we first meet;
eye to eye.
Sorrow lingers behind
your smile and the soul calls
to be embraced for a while.
Two birds soar outside the
bunkhouse door;
I see them take wing and fly
over the horizon,
over the trees,
over the silvery lake,
over the rooftops and
out beyond the night breeze
toward a single star that lights
this evening sky.
You cry and sleep alone,
and yet your time has come
to begin a journey of your own;
we are in Divine territory.

You can give without loving but you cannot love without giving.

—Victor Hugo, *Les Misérables*

Have You Been Hit On this Christmas?

The morning felt scattered. I was running late and I drove into the church parking lot sliding through the six inches of snow that had fallen overnight. Nothing was plowed. I grumbled. Grabbing my random things, I slid from my seat to the snowy carpet and slammed the door behind me. I was rummaging for the keys to the church door when I saw him walking toward me. He was a dark figure, tall and thin, wearing a long, black coat that was ripped under the arm and had no buttons. He wore a tattered watch cap and canvas sneakers. He had no gloves and no teeth. I knew him from a previous encounter.

I thought to myself, "Oh no. Not now. I don't have any small bills to give him." I knew it was what he wanted. I tried to pretend he wasn't there and walked determinedly toward the steps to the side door. I heard him call to me in a raspy voice. "Hey . . . Hey . . . lady . . . wait . . ." Was that God calling me? Not now.

I turned to him and we recognized each other. I had given him some money earlier in the fall when the weather was warm and I had a few dollars in my pocket. It wasn't a hassle. Now it's a hassle. I told him I didn't have any money. That was a lie. I had a twenty-dollar bill in my wallet.

I started to walk away from him and darned if my heart didn't pump out a little bit more love. And that conscience sitting on the tip of my shoulder said to me *"But it's Christmas!"* So I stopped and looked back at him. He had a scruffy grey and black beard and blurry dark eyes that squinted from the wind-driven snow. He didn't smile at me and his mouth was now shut so I couldn't see his missing teeth. I wondered who he might have been years ago. He actually reminded me of one of the kings in my Christmas nativity set.

"I've got some loose change in my car and I'll give it to you." He stood behind me as I unlocked the door and reached over and grabbed for the handful of change. "Here." I put the fistful of coins into the palm of his hand and our skin touched. He was cold and his hands were dry and chapped. "I don't know how much this is but you should get a cup of coffee out of it." He thanked me and walked away with his coat flapping in the wind.

I thought about him off and on that day. I had to reconcile with myself about not giving him the twenty. During lunch break I stopped at a drive-through for coffee. I reached into the car cup for some change before I remembered I had given it away. All I had was the twenty-dollar bill. I mentioned to the attendant that I had just given all my loose change away to a homeless guy. She handed me my coffee and said, "Well, only God knows what he'll do with it."

A FORGIVENESS MANTRA*

I am sending you loving kindness.
I am forgiving you
I wish you peace
I wish you health
I wish you happiness
I am letting go of the pain we have given one another.
I have carried it a long time and
now I will let it go.

**A mantra is a statement or prayer that can help relieve difficult feelings about people or events. Keep the mantra in your pocket or nearby, and say it often throughout the day. You can create your own mantras. They are good medicine for you and the universe.*

Perhaps the worst thing about suffering is that it finally hardens the hearts of those around it.

—Gloria Steinem, *Outrageous Acts and Everyday Rebellions*

A Moment

I walked into my bedroom after taking a shower this morning. I was clean, in fresh clothes, ready for the day. I walked past the front window and noticed a man standing at the side of my driveway, leaning on the trunk of the sycamore tree. He seemed distressed. He was wearing jeans, a long-sleeved shirt over a dark green tee shirt, and a black bandana around his head. He leaned his tall body forward and vomited. I watched a little longer, wondering if I should call an emergency vehicle for him. He heaved a few more times and then took a tissue from his pocket and wiped his mouth, the inside of each nostril, and his eyes. As I watched him, I wished I had some magical power to make him feel better. I thought perhaps he was dealing with cancer and the effects of chemotherapy. I spoke to God, "Can you send him some relief?"

The image of this man—this stranger, leaning against the tree, vomiting in the driveway—took away my feeling of comfort. My compassion for him pulled me from my place in the world into his place in the world. This is what so many people I have known and will come to know have to struggle with.

He put the tissue back into his pocket, straightened up, and walked away, leaving only the memory of his body against the tree and a stream of vomit trickling down the driveway into the street. I want to see him healed, strong, living the life he thought he'd have when he was twenty. All we have is this moment, and then the next moment and maybe the moment after that. We don't know when the moments will run out. I send peace and compassionate thoughts to this man who stepped into my moment.

THINKING OF JULIAN*

I stand in a cold doorway
forehead against the windowpane
lead framed, arched doors
bricks from centuries past
and I am thinking of Julian;
The solace of her cell
people walking by
dodging the plague
some stopping to ask
her why God was so angry.
The breath from my lips fogs
the glass and figures still pass.
Could she be thinking about me?

**Julian of Norwich was an English anchoress and a noted Christian mystic and theologian. Her* Revelations of Divine Love, *written around 1395, is the first book in the English language known to have been written by a woman.*

When Love comes suddenly and taps
on your window, run and let it in but first,
shut the door of your reason.

—Rumi, *Rumi: Hidden Music*

Learning to Love Like They Do in Heaven

I'VE BEEN THINKING LATELY about love and how I love others and how they love me. I've been thinking about the restrictions I put on love: who I can love and who I sort of can love and who I maybe should not love, although the latter seems to rub against the grain of my religious teachings. Perhaps the mystery is how much I can love someone or just exactly how I show my love for another, or how, out of fear, I don't show my love at all.

Pope Francis kissing the feet of young women prisoners is an example, I think, of how they must love one another in heaven—with no restrictions.

When I have loved someone so very dearly here on earth, and they pass on to the next journey before me, they are immediately with those whom they have loved before me. And I find other people to love, perhaps even as much as I loved them. What, then, will our love for one another be like when we all gather together in the same "other" place? Someone once said that when we "cross over" we take with us all the love everyone ever had for us, even those we might never have known.

Jesus had a special way to love people. It didn't matter whether they were men or women, or young or old, or sick or healthy, or whatever else they were. Those who follow his example are called to this "Christ-way-to-love." Scripture says it is in loving God first that we learn to love others, and ultimately to love ourselves.

I think this kind of love is how I love my spouse, all my children, my parents, the parent I never knew, the brother and sister I never knew. The love I have for my best friend or the neighbor who played jacks on the front porch with me when I was a child. The love for my art teacher who told me never to be afraid to share my feelings, and my grandmother who loved me just because she knew I needed it. Can we start this love here and now and then fully and fearlessly become that love in heaven?

Whatever this love is, and however we learn to share it with one another, it should be a part of our life right now, on this earth, at this moment. I want to love like they do in heaven . . . now, so when I get there I'll know exactly how to do it.

WOODEN CHAIRS

(A Strawberry Island Poem)

In the silent breakfast
I am acutely aware of the sound
of a water machine bubbling
like a brook that slides down its
glassy mountain sides.
We are told to cherish the quiet of
this time and mindfully eat our food.
Once in a while a clang of silverware
hits the dish or stirs the coffee in a cup.
There is a cough, a shift in the creaky
wooden dining room chairs that sit flat on
the hardwood floor, aged and scratched
over years of wear from monastic feet,
or in my case, the lonesome pilgrim
come to face her indulgences.
As I chew this spoonful of cereal
I must think about the grains and where
they have grown, who has harvested them,
where they were processed, made into
small little shapes that float in milk.
Breathing in . . . small shapes of cereal,
breathing out . . . bubbling water in a tank.
Then gentle Mary stands and bumps her chair.
I see it fall in slow motion, first to the side,
then straight back, and down with a thundering
roar to the sturdy, scraped brown floor.

Everything stops, everyone looks up at
startled, sweet Mary now standing in awe of the chair.
Mary likes to mindfully walk around the
grassy front yard, methodically maneuvering
each building, each small garden and rock.
Buildings and gardens do not fall when touched.
Wooden chairs do fall.

Now I lay me down to sleep;
I pray the Lord my soul to keep.
If I should die before I wake
I pray the Lord my soul to take.

—TRADITIONAL CHRISTIAN PRAYER

Prayer

I REMEMBER BEING AFRAID of thunder storms as a child. I remember waking up in the middle of the night during one such barrage of noise and light that so frightened me I walked down the hallway to my mother's bedroom and stood watching her sleep. Perhaps I thought I could think her awake. But she slept soundly, so I tapped her gently on the arm with my finger. I can still see her face as she looked up at me with a start. "What's wrong?" she asked.

"I'm afraid of the thunder," I replied with very little drama, as I have always been somewhat protective of my emotions and often give the impression of being an uncannily calm person in a storm. This calm outside display has led therapists and doctors who are not intuitive to see me as being perfectly fine when on the inside I might be raging. So, of course, my mother said to me, "Go back to bed and say a prayer and you will be fine." And I did and I was.

I have another memory of being afraid of the dark and my mother coming in to sit with me by my bed. She said all I had to do was pray and I would not be afraid. She taught me a prayer about guardian angels who would watch over me. To this day, I still think of that moment during fearful times and find comfort in it. I don't know if the simple act of a child's prayer is something that would always be comforting, though it worked perfectly well those two nights, and probably many other nights of now forgotten childhood trauma and fear. I came to believe that God was listening to me and I would be fine if I prayed.

The Catholics seem to have categorized prayer the most, with prayers of petition, prayers of absolution, tons of prayers for all kinds of occasions; so many I won't go into them. I was raised Catholic and can still remember learning my prayers, especially the ones I needed to know when I went into that tall wooden box with the velvet curtain to tell the priest I had chewed gum at mass and lied to a nun. "Say five Hail Mary's, my child!"

Over the years I have studied various methods of prayer. Centering prayer, Ignatius prayer, Lectio Divina, walking prayer, chanting, imaging, praying through art and music, and even sweat lodge prayers. But I must say the most simple and efficient prayer for me consists of stopping what I'm doing and taking time to be with God. Someone once said that all God wants from us is simply our presence. We don't have to pray or talk or even think. I do believe that is probably the most perfect way of prayer.

And I thank my mother for teaching me that simple act—that all I have to do is say a prayer and go back to sleep.

ISLAND DREAMS

(A Strawberry Island Poem)

There is an island floating
somewhere between here and there,
where tiny green ferns shoot up like
fairy thistles along a forest path;
where birds perch and sing
Glory to God like the national
anthem at a ball game,
and where trees forever loom
like mothers with welcoming arms
to those seeking the solace of home.
Where crabs meet their fateful end
as food for gulls and other creatures
of a lake never ending its enchanted
flow over rocks (some just right for skipping).
Where spiders spin enormous webs in
doorways, between screened windows,
under wooden steps and along deep, green
pathways which lead into places of mystery.
Where a stone shrine curves a carved way
and blesses an open field, so if you stop,
you may greet the woman, much like yourself,
or perhaps like your own mother who once
cradled you in her arms, then loved you
enough to let you go.
This is an island of great retreat,
of consolation and rest, of finding

acceptance and knowledge.
Where you can sit and be still with
all that surrounds you.
Swallows greet each day in monumental flight,
sweeping air currents to new journeys.
Loons and mergansers fill a small cove
with gentle understandings of what is truly
important at this moment in time.
But most of all it is God's face in those
you meet along the way that truly draws
you nearer to the inner voice you now
know as yourself.

The future is something that everyone reaches at the rate of sixty minutes an hour, whatever he does, whoever he is.

—C.S. Lewis, *The Screwtape Letters*

How To Do Nothing

The Advent practice for the day asks that I "sit in my cell for a half hour and do nothing." I can do this. It's 1:00 PM. I start by sitting and looking at the tops of the bare trees out the balcony door window that is in my study. I watch the tips of the branches sway in the wind at the backdrop of an all gray sky. Misty rain speckles the glass on the door. I listen to the tinnitus in my right ear. It is on high pitch but doesn't seem to matter. A few minutes pass.

Then I hear a voice from the next room: "Your cell phone is ringing." I attempt to ignore this proclamation, but the urge to know who is calling seems greater than my urge to do nothing. I'll go make a cup of tea. That will help me do nothing. I make my tea and find my cell phone. The call was from an online guidance counselor about my degree program. It was important and I note what she said on a sheet of paper, then go back to sit in my "cell." Maybe I should write a short email to the counselor to say I got her call. This takes about twenty minutes because I have to search the internet for some information I want to share with her.

Now my tea is cold, but it's okay. I look out at the tree tops again. Everything is as I left it a half hour ago. Too bad—I could be done by now, but I'm starting all over. I observe darker lower clouds passing overhead that look like smoke from a fire. There was a comment about "fire" in today's Advent practice. I know the usual advice: when on fire, "stop, drop, and roll" and stop any frantic motion that fans the flames. I can do that. It will put out the fire in my brain.

Suddenly my spouse charges in and announces, "I've finally finished the eulogy! Want to hear it?" Why yes . . . of course I do! She is a minister and is so good at writing these things. And so another twenty minutes pass. But I can still do this meditation practice. I close my door and lock myself in. It's 2:00 PM. I stop fanning the flames. In the world outside somewhere, I hear a fire engine.

I take two in-shell peanuts that I was keeping for the backyard squirrel from my breast pocket and eat them. I put the shells back in my pocket. I continue to look out the window and try to get the crushed peanuts out from between my teeth with my tongue. I methodically chew the little bits that are left and swallow them. There is cold air coming in from around the door sill. The wind continues to shake the tops of the trees and pull the dark smokey clouds across the sky. I close my eyes and try to shut it out. At arm's reach, I grab the blanket off the rocking chair and drape myself, head to foot.

Thoughts begin to creep into my mind. Those few grumpy people who are disgruntled with me for one reason or another. Why do they bother me at this very moment? Send them away. I feel the soreness in my muscles since I've been wearing a FitBit, and walking and exercising more. Send it away! I can almost still feel the cortisone shot that entered my left knee earlier this week. Send it away! And that tinnitus is still blaring. Send it all away. I still chew on tiny pieces of peanut that have stuck between my teeth. This is a mixed blessing; it keeps my mind from coming up with new thoughts that I will only have to send away.

"Are you there, God? Don't you want to say something?" No answer.

Sometimes all God wants is our presence. I stay with this thought for a long while. Then a memory comes to mind of my first time in centering meditation that was also supposed to last a half hour. It was during my spiritual direction training, when one of the other students fell asleep and started snoring. There were about six of us in the room and I remember opening one eye just a crack to see if there were any reactions. The snorer was slumped on the couch and those around him were seated upright with tiny grins at their lips. I remember how the time seemed to pass. Just like now, unfazed by all the interruptions.

I look at the clock on the wall and it's 2:36 PM. I think I did it.

NOT SPEAKING AT LAST

(A Strawberry Island Poem)

I am
in silence,
at last.
You laugh, for all
along you knew
I talked too much.
I walk in silence
from my room
to the dining hall.
People chatter,
I do not.
I listen and hear
the words, the sighs,
the laughs and sometimes
the cries that seem more
evident now that I am still.
I do not talk;
I watch the faces,
the hands clasping cups
or resting gentle on
wooden, green tables.
I see movements,
some quick, some slow,
some precise and fastidious,
scraping crumbs from plates.
I quietly leave and walk

about the lawns, feeling
the grass press down under my shoes.
Lake waves gently curl
and splash along rocks
at the shoreline; songbirds
sweetly sing at the top of trees
that sway in the summer wind.
When I am completely still,
not speaking,
not thinking,
not doing,
that is when God speaks
and fills my heart.

If your compassion does not include yourself, it is incomplete.

—ATTRIBUTED TO SIDDARTHA GAUTAMA, THE BUDDHA

Compassion for One

I RECENTLY WENT TO visit a friend in the hospital who was diagnosed with a heart ailment. She wore a monitor around her neck, and as we talked I saw her heart rate move up into the eighties and when she was quiet it lowered into the seventies. I don't know if all hearts do this. Not many of us wear monitors throughout the day but I bet if we did our heart rate would rise with our stress and lower in our silence.

I asked my friend if she had a mantra to recite when she was feeling worried or frightened. It often helps our bodies to relax when we reassure ourselves that things will be okay, that even at this moment we can move into a personal way of healing. This kind of healing doesn't always mean complete physical restoration, but momentary peace and quiet. This in itself is healing, for it is where the comfort of God lies, or whatever Higher Power in which you put your faith.

I found a meditation about being kind to yourself by Kristin Neff, associate professor of educational psychology at the University of Texas at Austin. Neff does research in the field of self-compassion and has written a book about her work.[1] This meditation[2] is a three-step contemplation exercise that offers a way to bring compassion to yourself through affirmation when you are feeling badly. The process involves putting your hands on your heart and

1. Neff, *Self-Compassion.*

2. Neff, "Self-Compassion," Written Exercise 2.

feeling the warmth, breathing deeply, and then speaking these words out loud or silently to yourself in a warm and caring way:

This is a moment of suffering.
Suffering is a part of life.
May I be kind to myself in this moment.

When doing meditation or mantras it is important to know that you can change any of the words to fit your personal needs. Depending on how you feel, you might change the first sentence to say This is a moment of pain, or a moment of sadness, or grief, or anger. You are recognizing that this is a feeling that is very much centered in your body and you are holding it, being at one with it. You might also place your hand(s) on any part of you that feels pain or discomfort.

The second sentence addresses the fact that the emotion or feeling you are having is legitimate and is "a part of life." You are not the only one who experiences these feelings, emotions, pains. Neff says this "is a part of the shared human experience."

The last sentence encourages you to be kind to yourself, to take care of that part of you that hurts, to give yourself the love and attention you need when others are perhaps being unkind or unforgiving, or in the case of hospitalization, are busy doing "to you," when what you need is reassurance or a hug. You might say to yourself, "May I give myself the compassion I need." Many turn to God or a Higher Power during these times, and if we think about the Oneness of all things, then perhaps our taking care of ourselves in this way is God within.

I once shared a similar mantra with a spiritual directee, and when I asked how it worked for her she said it was too long to remember. I understand this, as I often want something short and quick that I can use in the moment of driving, or of being confronted with any adversarial situation—something simple enough to repeat a few times until my heart rate and tension stabilizes. I offer this: I give myself the compassion I need in this moment. All is well.

IF JESUS WROTE POEMS:

That Morning

The sun rises red over the orchard;
My friends are still asleep beside me.
I hear their deep and unaffected breathing.
I feel anxious in this cold morning breeze.
A gray dove calls to the sky and its song
is mournful. The tune floats softly over
the tops of olive branches, and falls like
dry dust upon my tender ears.
Like a family lost on a journey together,
these men do not think I know where I am going.
I've asked them to follow me
but I fear they have lost faith in my navigation.
It is only God that knows my mind, my heart.
I would flee if I could but I am beholden to stay.
Sing little dove of the morning;
Sing me a song of comfort.

In the Temple

The temple is dark.
There is this smell
of damp stone and earth.
Along the side walls are
cracks where bits
of sunlight stream

across the floor.
It comes and finds me,
this light,
as I sit alone
breathing and praying
alone in the dark.

My Mother's Hand

In the crowd I am so small;
I am so lost, and so alone.
I reach out in my fear
for my mother's hand
and it is always there;
taking my flesh to her fingers,
wrapping her safe love
around me like the
walls of a sacred temple.

My Father's Gift

My father taught me
how to make a table.
The olive wood is planked
and honed smooth.
I feel the grain
beneath my calloused fingers
yet in my mind's eye
I still see the tree
ripe with fruit,
green and fresh and
plenty for all.

Heaven goes by favor. If it went by merit, you would stay out and your dog would go in.

—Attributed to Mark Twain

The Heart of Morgan

There are some stories worth telling and this is one. It's the story of how one moment in time can change the direction of your life. It's not my story, but that of my friend Nancy and her beloved therapy dog, Morgan, who has left this life, but not Nancy's memory and heart.

Morgan was a Shetland Sheepdog, also known as a Sheltie, and Nancy said he had the face of an angel. From the early days of puppy-hood it was evident that Morgan had a spiritual quality that was almost humanlike. He seemed to know how people were feeling and genuinely cared about them.

Nancy told of how her father had lain in hospice, unresponsive until a volunteer brought in their therapy dog to visit him. As the dog's warm fur touched her father's hand, he responded ever so slightly to the dog's presence. This was that moment: she knew then that Morgan's place was doing hospice work and that she would join him in the journey.

Morgan was trained and certified as a therapy dog, and together, he and Nancy spent many years as volunteers with Lifetime Care Hospice in Rochester, New York. Nancy told me about a visit with a dying woman, who like her father, was not responsive. She sat at her bedside and Morgan lay next to the woman, who opened her eyes and put her arms around the dog, gently stroking his warm fur. The space became holy. She died shortly thereafter.

Many warm and loving memories were shared between these two volunteers. Their presence filled the last moments in peoples' lives with comfort and peace. Spirit moves among us in the most astounding ways. Morgan was more than a companion and therapy dog. He was a spiritual presence in the way his heart touched the hearts of others.

In my creche set that I put up on our mantle each Christmas, I have a small ceramic Sheltie dog. It's old, and the paint on it is chipped. I never paid it much attention until I heard the story of Morgan. Sometimes I place the dog by the shepherds and sometimes I place it by the figures of Joseph and Mary as they travel to Bethlehem by donkey. This year I will put the little dog in the manger next to the empty cradle that waits for a child to be born. I will name it Morgan.

CASTING SEEDS

(A Strawberry Island Poem)

Are your seeds cast out along the asphalt of
city streets, blown under cars and feet of
those who never stop to notice you?
Are your seeds cast out along the rocks
that line the outside of buildings and walkways
where boundaries and walls lock you in or lock
you out of some exclusive knowledge that says
you will never fit into their mold?
Do you hold onto the seeds that fall from thorn
trees, lest they germinate the soil you cultivate
and procreate into something hateful with sharp
edges causing your life to bleed?
Cast your seeds, gentle one,
into the rich soil of love and tolerance;
into the earth of acceptance and desire;
into the mindfulness of each moment we know
we are awake and on fire with life;
into the garden we planted with seeds saved
from asphalt, rocks, walls, locks and sharp ignorance.
Cast your seeds into the bed of sacred ground.

Bibliography

The Bhagavad Gita. Translated by Eknath Easwaran. New York: Vintage, 2000.

Bourgeault, Cynthia. *The Wisdom Jesus: Transforming Heart and Mind—A New Perspective on Christ and His Message*. Boston: Shambhala, 2008.

Chernoff, Mindy Tatz. "Animals, Spiritual Direction, and Prayer." *Presence Magazine: An Int'l. Journal of Spiritual Direction* 17, 1 (March 2011) 39–43.

Collins, Billy. *Nine Horses*. New York: Random House, 2003.

Eckhart. *Meister Eckhart: The Essential Sermons, Commentaries, Treatises, and Defense*. Translated by Edmund Colledge and Bernard McGinn. Classics of Western Spirituality. Mahwah, NJ: Paulist Press, 1981.

Ekaku, Hakuin. "Yabukoji." In *The Zen Master Hakuin: Selected Writings*. Translated by Philip B. Yampolsky. New York: Columbia University Press, 1971.

Harrer, Heinrich. *Seven Years in Tibet*. Translated by Richard Graves. New York: Jeremy P. Tarcher, 2009.

Helminski, Kabir, ed. *The Pocket Rumi Reader*. Boston: Shambhala, 2001.

Johnsen, Linda. *Hindusim: The Complete Idiot's Guide*. 2nd ed. New York: Alpha, 2009.

Johnston, William. *Mystical Theology: The Science of Love*. London: HarperCollins, 1996.

Kornfield, Jack. *Meditation for Beginners*. Boulder, CO: Sounds True, 2004.

LaJeunesse, E.J. *Strawberry Island in Lake Simcoe*. Toronto: Basilian Press, 1962.

Lamott, Anne. *HELP, THANKS, WOW: The Three Essential Prayers*. New York: Riverhead, 2012.

Mandino, Og. "The Scroll Marked II." In *The Greatest Salesman in the World*. New York: Bantam, 1983.

Markides, Kyriacos C. *The Mountain of Silence: A Search for Orthodox Spirituality*. An Image Book. New York: Doubleday, 2002.

Moore, Thomas. *Care of the Soul*. New York: HarperCollins, 1992.

Neff, Kristin. "Self-Compassion." https://self-compassion.org/exercises/exercise-2-self-compassion-break/

———. *Self-Compassion: The Proven Power of Being Kind to Yourself*. New York: William Morrow, 2015.

Welton, Robert. "Be Your Own Light." https://www.beliefnet.com/faiths/buddhism/be-your-own-light.aspx.

———. *Be Your Own Light*. Santa Barbara, CA: ReflectLight, 2012.

www.ingramcontent.com/pod-product-compliance
Lightning Source LLC
LaVergne TN
LVHW012334100826
845148LV00017B/2285

* 9 7 9 8 3 8 5 2 6 9 2 3 5 *